My Friend
My Lover
My Husband

A Triumphant Experience
Dealing with Crack Cocaine

Foreword by Dr. Terry M. Turner – Pastor

Avis Lamb Brown

This book is dedicated
to
Carrie (Grand Momma) Lamb, deceased,
Lenora (Big Momma) Lamb
&
John and Vyrle (Pop & Granny) Brown, deceased
For their spiritual guidance while our family
struggled with crack addiction
"For we walk by faith, not by sight"
(2 Corinthians 5:7, NKJV).

Foreword

PROFESSOR AVIS BROWN, in the second edition of her autobiography book *My Friend, My Lover, My Husband*, reveals how unsettling marriage can become when lived outside of God's guidelines. In the Garden of Eden, Adam and Eve were married by God without having time for a courtship or an introduction—they were at once friends and lovers. In the beginning although the first couple was made perfect for each other, their marriage was filled with tragic events. Every married man and woman desires to have a spouse who will be a friend and lover. Marriage, as God designed, is intended to survive all the hardships life can produce. The greatest example of this is the married life of Adam and Eve. In weddings today, the bride and groom stand at the altar and make a commitment before God, family, and friends to stay together in marriage through sickness and health, for richer and poorer, forsaking all others until death parts them. But these newly married couples are blind to the heartbreaking trials life will bring their way with the person they love and have committed to endure the situations of life.

Brown, in a spirit of self-denial, battles old anxieties, memories, and pains to rewrite her story from a Christian perspective about a victim wife caught up in the African American drug culture. She has brought something new to her story after years of going through spousal drug recovery, mental healing, and finding God as the source of her strength. With an entirely different understanding of her past life, she is able to approach the story from the ways God was at work in all the drug-related difficulties created while her husband, James, was dependent on crack cocaine. Through God's grace, they are now loyal and active members of Mesquite Friendship Baptist Church where I pastor. They are busy as a couple and serve the Lord inside and outside of the church.

This book needed to be written and rewritten, and there is no one more capable than Brown. She is a woman who has lived through the issues of this book and came out victorious. The first edition was written in resentment and opposition from the view of a distressed wife who wanted all to know how her husband, through his drug use, was responsible for causing much pain in her life. Brown now writes about the early years of her marriage absent of anger and hostility—redirecting the emotions of a wounded wife who wanted vengeance on her husband for creating years of suffering for her and the children. She has taken the time to research and explain the physical and mental science of crack cocaine addiction in an effort to help others who are going through this same tragedy. In addition, her work will help others to understand how the mind and body are impacted during the time of chemical addiction. Brown's story is now filled with Bible verses and gives glory to God for the victories He gave to both her and James as they went through drug-related hardships to find their Christian faith.

This book will become a great contribution to African American marriages and families in danger of becoming extinct due to social risk factors. The leading cause for the destruction of these families and marriages is the negative perception of marriage among couples and their pre-marital decisions not to marry, but remain single. The crack cocaine epidemic within African American marriages and families has been the cause for many marital dysfunctions and dissolutions. In finding the strength to overcome the warfare of the drug culture, the Browns found God in the midst of their marriage and, unlike in the beginning, He has become the glue that keeps them together. Now take the time to get educated, angry, laugh, cry, and enjoy the testimony of how a determined wife found God and defeated the destructive risk factors within a marriage caught in the drug culture.

Dr. Terry M. Turner, Senior Pastor
Mesquite Friendship Baptist Church

Table of Contents

Books of the Bible Abbreviation
English Standard Version **(ESV)**
International Standard Version **(ISV)**
King James Version **(KJV)**
New Living Translation **(NLT)**
New American Standard Bible **(NASB)**
New International Version **(NIV)**
New King James Version **(NKJV)**

Introduction

MANY YEARS AGO, my family and I were caught in a worldly addiction that has been a part of society for many years. Consequently, the effect of this addiction on many families has been devastating, while trying to live the American dream that was instilled in my upbringing in the South as a child. The world we live in has so much to offer both positively and negatively. However, how could I prepare our family for what was ahead? What I did not understand was how a white powdered substance could change a person's behavior, appearance, and dependency.

Dealing with challenges in our marriage was expected, but how do you deal with an addiction that changes the face of how marriage is supposed to be? Who do you go to when your family is forced to deal with a loved one who is hooked on a substance that alters the plans on what a marriage should be? How do you raise children in such a negative environment while trying to shield them from the day-to-day shame and embarrassment? During this time in my life, I was too concerned with getting even with Lucious for his crack cocaine addiction.

The years of trial and error in my life of trying to manage an addiction which affected my family forced me to turn it over to my God. Because I realized I did not have the power to change anything or anyone in my life, I knew the Lord could. After reading this book, you will find out as I have, that my fight of dealing with an addicted family member was never mine to do alone. All I had to do was pray for daily guidance, deliverance, and believe God would take care of our family situation. *"Now faith is the substance of things hoped for, the evidence of things not seen" (**Hebrews 11:1, KJV**).*

Crack Cocaine User and Effects

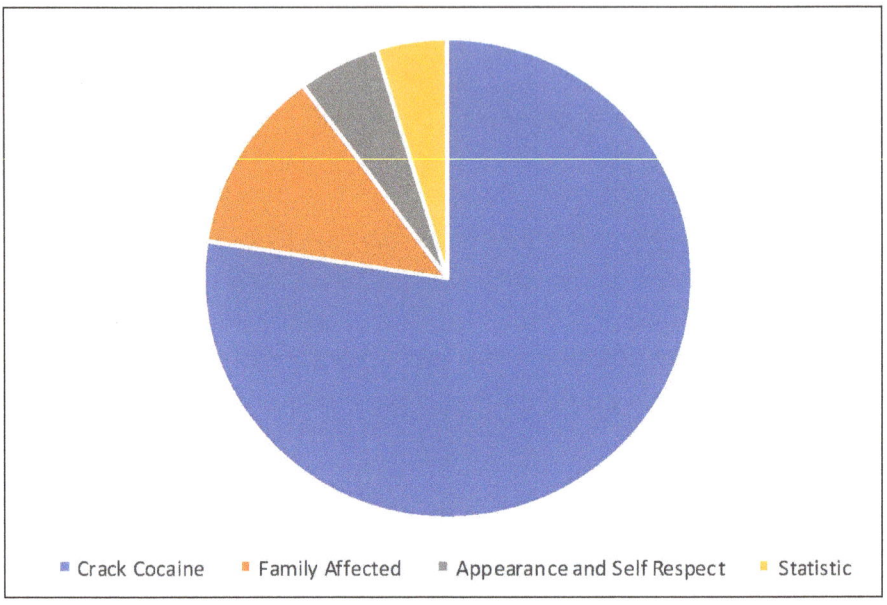

- Crack Cocaine
- Family Affected
- Appearance and Self Respect
- Statistic

*"For thou shalt worship no other god: for the LORD, whose name is Jealous, is a jealous God" (**Exodus 34:14, KJV**).*

*"You shall have no other gods before Me" (**Exodus 20:3, NKJV**).*

Selected historical years of Cocaine

- During the 1400s and earlier throughout South America, coca is believed to be a blessing from God.
- During the 1500s, Texas leaders would take 1/10 in levies taxes for the value of each crop of coca.
- During the 1800s, cocaine was removed from coca leaves and used as a painkiller for eye surgery.

- During the 1900s, one of the largest soft drink companies took coca out of its soft drink formula. The use of cocaine became popular along with freebase.
- During the 21ˢᵗ century, crack cocaine usage is still a drug of choice and is considered a recreational drug.

"And God said, Let the earth bring forth grass, the herb yielding seed, and the fruit tree yielding fruit after his kind, whose seed is in itself, upon the earth: and it was so" **(Genesis 1:11, KJV)**.

Crack

During the 1980s, a new drug word entered the vocabulary of people in the United States: **CRACK**. The only other drug that has received as much publicity as crack cocaine, is marijuana and it is now considered by many to be a "safe" drug. Crack is extremely dangerous. It is a more powerful form of cocaine—a cheaper, smokeable form developed in 1986 by drug dealers. However, unlike cocaine, crack kills. The name "crack" came from the crackling sound of the cocaine rock popping when users would heat and smoke it. The drug usage moved from the inner, more impoverished neighborhoods to businesses and social events throughout our society. Crack continues to cause danger to the family environment and finances while sweeping across the United States impacting society.

The crack epidemic started during the 1980's and 1990's remains a popular drug of choice today, despite the danger since it is inexpensive to make and purchase. Crack cocaine is cooked to a liquid, then smoked by the drug user rather than snorted. If smoked, it enters the bloodstream through the lungs and has a much stronger and dangerous effect on the brain. The craving overpowers the desire to seek periods of short-lived crack highs. Hence, the birth of crack addiction is formed. Many drug users pursue ways to purchase the drug with little or no regard as to how it is obtained to get the next high. The outcome of experiencing crack cocaine is addictive behavior and chemical dependency to the drug.

Sale of Crack Cocaine

Crack sales grew at a rapid speed because of the low cost compared to the price of cocaine. Drug users could receive the same effect they got from cocaine, but for a much lower price. As a reality there were considerable profits in selling crack. Due to the economic price tag, it generated new customers that were on the streets selling crack. It has attracted the attention of vicious criminals throughout the world. There are hundreds and, perhaps, thousands of crack houses in the United States today. These crack houses are private homes where cocaine is smuggled from Central and South America, converted into the crack, and sold. Crack gangs murder each other and, all too often, innocent men, women, and children. The amount of violence among dealers who fight to keep control of the areas in their part of town is known as their "turf." The violence among users is tremendous.

Since the white powdered substance can be smoked in a pipe, sniffed through the nostril, and swallowed. In addition to the problems of violence, crack, just like the cocaine that is snorted, can cause severe lung damage, not to mention a devastating dependence on the drug. Most users of the drug seek the feeling of intense pleasure, a high that occurs for a short period after taking crack cocaine. When the drug effect wears off, usually after 20 to 40 minutes, the users feel depressed and take another dose to regain that euphoria intense feeling. Some users reach a point where they continuously crave the drug. The long-term use of crack may cause some users to suffer depression and inability to hold a job because they are undependable workers. In addition, the purchase of crack cocaine has caused many deaths, family divisions and lost souls. Careers are damaged because addicts spend most of their money on drugs. *"For what does it profit a man, if he shall gain the whole world, and lose his own soul?"* **(Mark 8:36, KJV).**

Symptoms of Crack Cocaine

Crack can affect the mind and cause the addict to kill people who are perceived as enemies. If too much of the drug is used, it can stop the heart from pumping, and ultimately kill you. Crack causes sudden increases in the heart rate and blood pressure. Some crack users suffer from seizures or heart attacks while using crack. People on crack feel more alert, powerful, and their thinking process seems better and more clearer than usual. Occasionally, heightened anxiety, irritability, cravings, and fear occur instead of the expected high. Rumor has it that users can be rendered completely dysfunctional in a two or three-month period.

The use of cocaine, whether in its original form or transformed into the crack, is a significant drug problem spreading rapidly throughout the world. Today, we are forced to face the terrible truth about crack cocaine. This drug is becoming more and more popular among adolescents, and it is responsible for an alarming increase in the number of people seeking treatment for physical and emotional problems. It is one of the reasons many hospital emergency rooms are overcrowded and overwhelmed with drug-related cases. It is found almost anywhere—in schools, on the job, and on the streets—and can be sold for as little as five dollars a hit.

Bazooka (Basuco), an impure form of crack, can sell for just a couple of bucks. However, the initial cost is usually not the last. You begin to want more and more of the drug until you spend every cent you have. It is crucial—a matter of life and death—to understand the high risks involved in the crack use because an overdose will unfortunately result in death. Once you depend on crack or any illegal drug, the result is simple: **DEATH**. Apostle Paul says, *"Awake, O sleeper,"* the death Paul speaks of, is a spiritual death found in those who depend on crack cocaine as a way of life.

"Let no one deceive you with empty words, for because of these things the wrath of God comes upon the sons of disobedience. Therefore do not become partners with them; for at one time you were darkness, but now you are light in the Lord. Walk as children of light (for the fruit of light is found in all that is good and right and true), and try to discern what is pleasing to the Lord. Take no part in the unfruitful works of darkness, but instead expose them. For it is shameful even to speak

of the things that they do in secret. But when anything is exposed by the light, it becomes visible, for anything that becomes visible is light." Therefore, it says,

'Awake, O sleeper,
        and arise from the dead,
and Christ will shine on you.'

Look carefully then how you walk, not as unwise but as wise, making the best use of the time, because the days are evil. Therefore, do not be foolish, but understand what the will of the Lord is. And do not get drunk with wine, for that is debauchery, but be filled with the Spirit" (**Ephesians 5:6-18, ESV).**

Some Visual Signs of Crack Cocaine Users

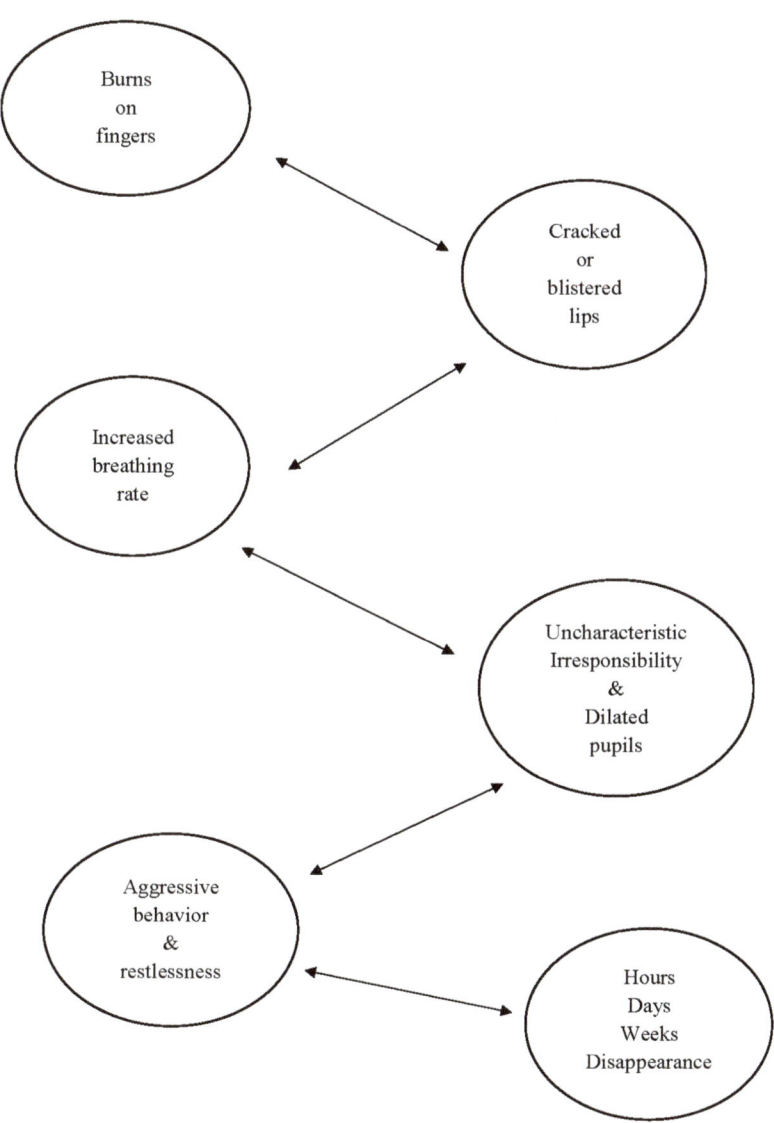

Crack/Crack Cocaine

Crack is a chemical substance that can cause changes
in the human body.

Crack cocaine is a white powdered substance.

Crack cocaine is an illegal drug in the United States.

Crack causes the user to lose interest in everything except getting
the next dose of the drug.

Crack gradually changes the chemistry of the abuser's body.

Crack causes a user to break laws and commit crimes to get money
to buy the illegal drug.

Crack is a more powerful form of cocaine.

Cocaine comes from the leaf of the Coca Plant.

*"Be sober, be vigilant; because your adversary the devil, as a roaring
lion, walketh about, seeking whom he may devour"* (**1 Peter 5:8, KJV**).

Crack Cocaine Process Map Flow

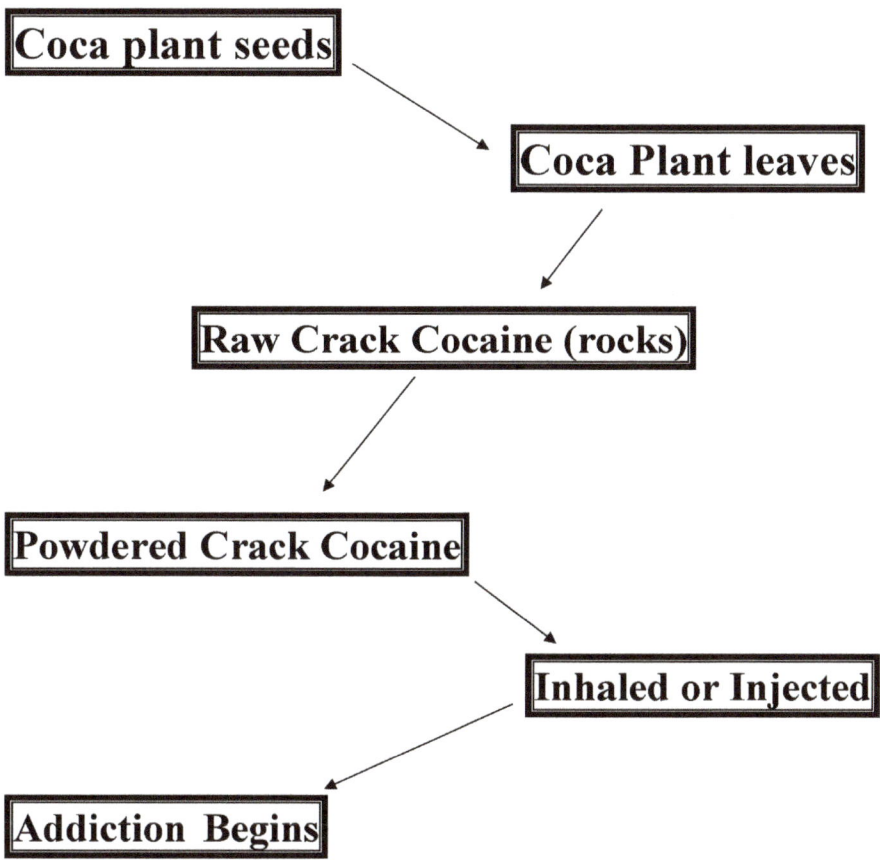

Coca plant seeds

Coca Plant leaves

Raw Crack Cocaine (rocks)

Powdered Crack Cocaine

Inhaled or Injected

Addiction Begins

"Like a city whose walls are broken through is a person who lacks self-control" ***(Proverbs 25:28, NIV).***

Crack Versus the Brain

YOUR **BRAIN** WITHIN your *mind* is the control center of your body. It sends out billions of electrical signals every day. The message speeds along from one nerve cell to the next until they reach every part of your body. However, crack is a stimulant. When crack is used, it speeds up the way the brain works and sends out too many electrical signals. The signals may cause a seizure, which means the brain's electrical messages have been mixed up. The body begins to shake all over and becomes stiff. Crack can also cause blood vessels of the brain to burst; this is called a "stroke" and can lead to brain damage or sudden death.

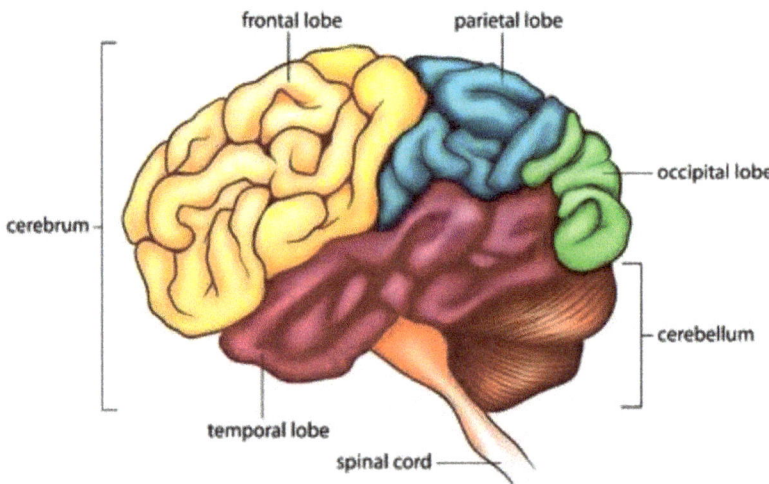

frontal lobe   parietal lobe

occipital lobe

cerebrum

cerebellum

temporal lobe

spinal cord

"Their end is destruction, their god is their belly, and they glory in their shame, with minds set on earthly things" **(Philippians 3:19, ESV).**

Crack Versus the Heart

THE **HEART** PUMPS blood to every part of the body, day and night. Inside the heart, is a particular area called the pacemaker; this keeps the heart pumping by sending out electrical signals to the heart muscles. The brain controls the pacemaker. Messages from the brain tell the pacemaker to speed up or slow down. When crack cocaine is used, the heart beats so fast that the muscles of the heart may become damaged. Using crack can lead to a heart attack or sudden death.

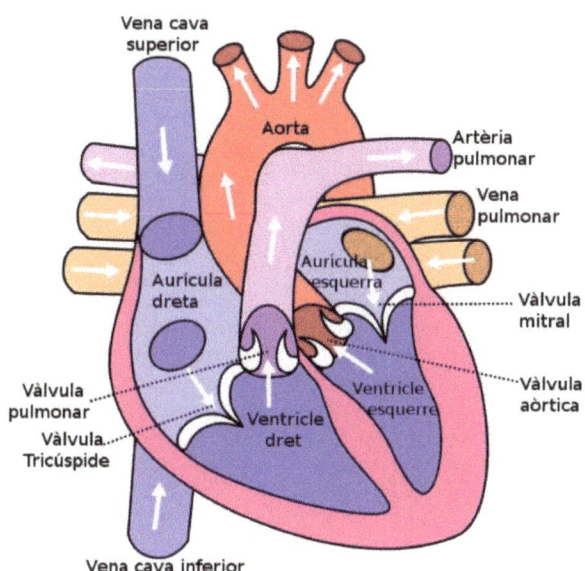

"And the peace of God, which surpasses all understanding, will guard your hearts and your minds in Christ Jesus" (**Philippians 4:7, ESV).**

Crack Versus the Lungs

OUR LUNGS **BREATHE** in the air we need to live, and then breathe out the air our bodies do not need. The oxygen enters the bloodstream, and the heart pumps it throughout the body. A unique control area in the brain sends out electrical signals to the lungs to let it know how fast and how deep to breathe. Crack use hurts the lungs and leads to shortness of breath, making it harder for the lungs to get oxygen into the blood. It also stops the brain from sending out those electrical signals that keep the lungs breathing. Continuous use of crack causes the lungs to stop working altogether and leads to sudden death.

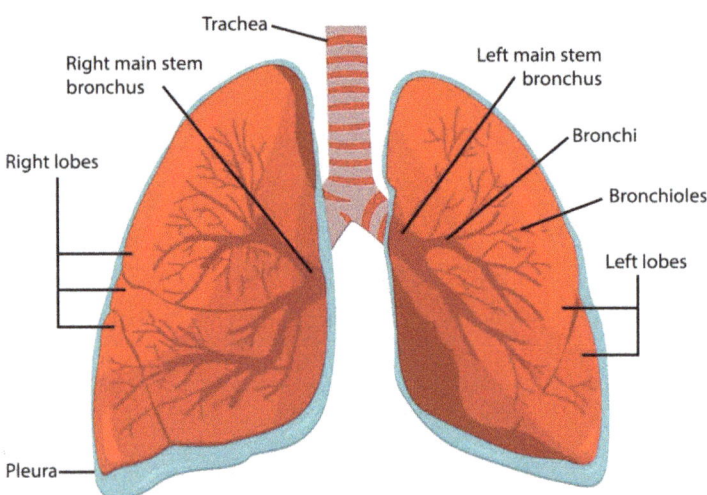

*"Jesus said to them again, 'Peace be with you. As the Father has sent me, even so I am sending you.' And when he had said this, he breathed on them and said to them, 'Receive the Holy Spirit' (**John 20:21-22, ESV**)*

Crack Add-diction

DO YOU EVER wonder about the drugs which exist in our society around you and your family? Are you curious enough about what it does and why people use them? More and more people are using crack and do not have the willpower to stop. Many of our loved ones use crack "as" their drug of choice. Do not wait until it hits close to home, and then try to do something about it. Strike now:

Strike now because crack kills!

The story you are about to read is not fiction, not make-believe. It reveals how a family was forced to deal with a crack addict as a friend, a lover, and a husband. When you choose to ignore the matter and wait until it is too late, some of the ten examples listed below will possibly be the outcome of your individual life or family life.

1) Car + Crack = Zero
2) Bank Account + Crack = Zero
3) Job + Crack = Zero
4) Spouse + Crack = Zero
5) Children + Crack = Zero
6) House + Crack = Zero
7) Respect + Crack = Zero
8) Dignity + Crack = Zero
9) Salvation + Crack = Zero
10) Crack + Crack = Death

"But seek ye first the kingdom of God, and his righteousness; and all these things shall be added unto you" (**Matthew 6:33, KJV**).

My Resume of Life

By
Avis Lamb Brown

Poe Poor Po, a victim of welfare aid
In the project of life where we all played
Struggling from day to day
Bang! Bang! Join a gang,
Childhood is a joke, struggling to cope,
Grandmother's rules,
Father's drinking blues,
Father dies, my question is why?
Sisters and brothers spread far and near,
I don't understand to offer a tear,
A mother forced to raise children of eight,
Black and single, a lonely mate,
Two, Four, Six, Eight,
Living together in a southern state,
Grandmother withdrawn
After Father had gone,
I look up to thee and
Think of what he has seen,
How my blessed Poe Poor Po life has been?
"You will always have the poor among you,
but you will not always have me" **(Matthew 26:11, NLT).**

My Friend, My Lover, My Husband - Secular Issues

My Friend

Lucious and I met and became a couple on the college campus where we learned about Christ and the family. Dating during the late 1970's while attending a Christian college in East Texas was normal because that's what a lot of the students did find a husband or wife. Family values were a top priority among families, and you were expected to represent your family name respectfully. Our fathers and mothers shared their values with us as they were shared with them by their fathers and mothers. Setting family values were necessary and essential and were passed down from generation to generation. With the utmost respect, the man held the woman as the lead person in decision making for the family and couple while dating/courting.

My Lover

During our dating or courtship experience, we did things that were considered secular or without a Christian basis. We were 'sowing our oats' as the old people would call it. Courting was a process of getting to know each other as a friend. After courting for an extended period, we both decided to become lovers. Falling in love and not wanting to be without each other, enjoying what life had to offer, going to clubs, drinking, and enjoying our friends in the fast lane. Lucious was raised up in a two-parent household in a small Missouri town, I was raised up by a single mom in the city. We enjoyed having fun and did it quite often when we were in college. Lucious and I took trips together in the car given to him by his parents. We shared exciting times enjoying each other during three years of college and decided to get married after graduation.

My Husband

When we got married, Lucious' role was the head of the house as well as an instant father, I submitted to Lucious and then the household duties. We were often told to live the American dream as we continued our lives together as a family. However, life challenges as a couple began to happen. Working on our American dream away from each other while working on our jobs, temptation began to creep into our marriage. During the beginning of our relationship in Texas, we were surrounded by like-minded people who were familiar with our Lord and savior Jesus Christ and upheld college standards. Now that we were away from that Christian environment and thrust into a new environment faced with different beliefs and values, we were forced to deal with something we had never experienced before. What exactly is the American dream, is it the right or wrong idea for our family, is it a goal friends, lovers, and husband/wife work together as a marriage vision? *"And we know that in all things God works for the good of those who love him, who have been called according to his purpose"* **(Romans 8:28, NIV)**.

Mixed Signals of a Crack Addict

LUCIOUS AND I dated while in college in Texas. We decided after graduating from school that Lucious would join the United States Air Force. His first duty station was at Little Rock Air Force base in Arkansas. During his first tour in the Air Force, Lucious had an accident and was discharged from the military due to medical reasons. We had to adjust in dealing with him having to take medication for the rest of his life and moving to another new state to live. On May 12, 1985, we decided to move our family to Dallas, Texas. We both looked forward to the move and each had a job waiting for us in Dallas. Lucious would work the day shift at a company near our new home, and I would work the night shift for a company downtown. We had two lovely boys: Jr., our oldest, was eleven, and Steven was turning five.

When we first moved, we did not know anything about Dallas except that we fell in love with the city during our visits while in college. We worked together like any family does by providing for each other and the boys. During our days off together, we would take the boys to the movies and maybe to the nearest lake for a picnic. Back when Lucious and I were dating, we always went on picnics. Once we got married, we continued to work on our marriage hoping to keep the home fires burning. When Lucious was at work, I would go to his job to have lunch with him, and when I was working, he and the boys would come to my job to eat dinner with me. Since things seemed to be okay with my family, or so I thought, I began to dedicate more of my time in developing a management career. What I was doing was tearing my marriage apart. The more I advanced in my career and the more successful I became, the more my head was swelling. Sure, I was successful at my job, but I put my career before my family. They were slowly becoming secondary in my life. My husband had a good job, but my career took off like a rocket, and I had to keep up. Even though I shared my success with my family, something was missing communication began to lack between us. He never let on to me how he felt. He was becoming frustrated and having problems with our marriage. I now wish the Bible could have helped him. The Apostle Paul says, *"Husbands, love your wives, and be not bitter against them"* (**Colossians 3:19, KJV).**

I remembered while growing up in Liberty City Florida, I had always dreamed of joining the Army, so I did. I joined the Army National Guard in Little Rock, Arkansas, and transferred to Dallas. Lucious was in the Air Force and also stationed in Little Rock, Arkansas, but later discharged due to medical. After the move to Dallas I received my orders from the Army in Dallas and had to leave my family for about four months out of the year. We sent our boys to my mother and my husband was in Dallas all alone.

Thinking back, one of the most terrible things I ever had to do was leave my boys for those four months. At this point in my life, though, I just wanted to fulfill my childhood dreams. I did not think of the repercussions my dreams would cause my family and me. For two years, I served four months out of each year to complete my service training. Once training was finished, I was reunited with my husband and boys. I tried very hard to piece my loving family back together as we once were whole. And I thought I could do it. However, I could not do it alone. I eventually discovered that when I went off to work Lucious would leave them in the apartment all alone, with my oldest son in charge who was only eleven years old.

When I questioned Lucious about it, he told me he had things to do and places to go, and the boys would only be in the way. I said to him we had agreed to take part in the babysitting responsibilities, and he needed to live up to his part of that agreement. I remained concerned because we never resolved the problem. From that day forward, I kept a close eye on the boys. I called home at least five times a day while I was at work to make sure all was okay. Lucious forgot his role as head of the house. I began to depend more on the Word of God where Paul encourages family members caught up in life's trials, financial difficulties, and tribulations. *"But if any provide not for his own, and especially for those of his own house, he hath denied the faith, and is worse than an infidel" (1 Timothy 5:8, KJV).*

Months passed and my in-laws decided they were going to visit us around the Christmas holiday. I became very ill during their visit, so they ended up taking care of our boys the majority of the time because Lucious would leave for hours at a time without any explanation to anyone. My in-laws were always around when I needed help the most, and I am genuinely thankful for their support. As time went on, living with him not as husband and wife made us grow farther apart. We argued over simple little things that didn't make sense.

Sometimes while he was out, the telephone would ring. When I answered, the caller would hang up. At the time, I did not overthink those calls, believing they were probably just someone dialing the wrong numbers. I started putting little things together, but I refused to go looking. However, one day while I was home from work, a woman called to speak to Lucious. I told her he was not back and asked if she would like to leave a message. She answered, "No!" and hung up on me. It was apparent something was going on between this woman and my husband.

Instead of lashing out at Lucious with jealousy and anger, I started thinking about whether our marriage was worth fighting for, or if it would be better to leave him because of one telephone call. Then I thought to myself, do I get even, or do I get out? Instead of making a big deal out of my suspicions, I decided we would buy a home together and work on our marriage. I convinced him to join me in looking for a house. He agreed, partly out of the guilt he was feeling – at this point, it did not matter. I knew he was guilty of seeing another woman; his actions told me the whole story. Nevertheless, all I wanted to do was focus on getting what *I* wanted instead of getting revenge, and I knew how to get it. After all, I *am* the woman of the house. *"For the love of money is the root of all evil: which while some coveted after, they have erred from the faith, and pierced themselves through with many sorrows"* (**1 Timothy 6:10, KJV**).

As time went on, I started noticing a dramatic change in our savings account and found receipts for withdrawals only days apart. When I questioned Lucious about it, he naturally had an excuse. Being in love, but also feeling hurt at the same time, I did not lash out in anger. I held my head high and blocked out the hurt and focused even more on taking care of the boys and me. At this time, he did not matter to me. I began to drown my sorrows in my work, focusing on being promoted, all at the cost of our marriage. I wanted a house, regardless of the betrayal my spouse was putting on our marriage.

We looked around North Dallas, West Dallas, and then we stumbled upon a home being built in East Dallas. We applied for the house, months later we heard from the mortgage company. We were approved and had an appointment to sign the papers for our new home. While waiting on the home approval I would drive by the house, even if I was not in the area, because once I saw it, I knew I had to have it. I would go by to see the house being built and what type of neighborhood environment we were moving into, especially when it was rainy, sunny, night, or day, We both seemed to be excited, or so I thought. Instead, it was only the boys who shared the joy of buying a new home with me. During the next couple of days, while moving into our new house, and during the move, Lucious got lost a couple of times driving the U-Haul from the apartment to the house.

Once settled, I planted grass and ended up doing all of the yard work myself. As I think about it today, he did nothing to help. I was so wrapped up in getting a home that I continued to work to make my dream and my revenge a reality. After a couple of months in our new home, Lucious began to stay out until all hours of the night, and some nights he would not come home at all. Once again, the phone calls started with the caller always hanging up when I answered. One evening, a woman with a familiar voice called and asked to speak with Lucious. I asked her what she wanted with him, and she replied in a rude tone, "Who are you?" "Who is this?" I answered.

She then went on to say, Lucious told her he lived with his sister; I guess I was the sister. I introduced myself as his wife, not his sister, and politely asked her to quit calling my husband at this number again. After I hung up the phone, I started to snoop into Lucious' belongings. After I found the lady's name and telephone numbers at her job and home. I decided to call her back and left Lucious' name and a message to call him at home. Within minutes, the phone rang. Of course, it was the lady I had just called. Again, she asked to speak with Lucious. I told her he was not available. She said I was wrong because he had just called. I said, "No, he did not just call you. I called – his wife – and left his name."

I warned her that if she ever called my home again, I would go to her job and deal with her in person. Then I said, "Please, call my bluff." I did not hear from her again. I do not know if Lucious ever knew of our conversation, as he never said anything about it to me. I did, however, confront him about the phone hang-ups. He denied having ever given any woman our telephone number. I did not press the issue, but kept my eyes and ears opened from that point on. I refused to overlook the situation while still loving him. I know it was wrong because the Word of God tells us, *"Vengeance is Mine, and retribution, in due time their foot will slip; for the day of their calamity is near, and the impending things are hastening upon them"* (**Deuteronomy 32:35, NASB**).

Weeks later, Lucious got a call from his supervisor and was

instructed to take a polygraph test. I got the information second hand – better yet, I was told what Lucious wanted me to hear while he was on the telephone. He later said to me he was accused of stealing hubcaps from cars during work. This was also the place where he had met his girlfriend. I was perplexed, but cautious, because things were happening without any explanations. Lucious was terminated as a result, and somehow he managed to find another job as a security guard. He continued to stay out for days, and his whereabouts were unknown to me. When we first married, we both agreed that if one of us went out without the other, we would come home by 2:00 in the morning with plenty enough time to enjoy what was out there. When he finally made it home, I reminded him of this agreement. He denied it, of course, and I became more and more convinced that either he had someone else in his life or something else was going on.

A month passed, and Lucious was still staying out late. I started to realize I was not able to depend on him anymore for support. I became furious and fed up with his actions and confronted him again. This time, though, I was not going to accept his answer. Instead, I gave him an ultimatum. But what good did that do? Days passed, and I continued to focus on my boys and my job as a manager. My marriage to Lucious was breaking up into small pieces, and he did not seem to care. Nevertheless, I had responsibilities and a drive to fulfill my goals and dreams. Buying a home, in my mind, gave me a sense of security and was not just a fulfillment of my dreams it was *my* part of the American Dream. I found myself living for worldly moments, and not for God, *"Love not the world, neither the things that are in the world. If any man love the world, the love of the Father is not in him"* (**1 John 2:15, KJV**).

It had now been nine months since we bought our new home and Lucious was spending more time in the street than at the house. I did all the yard work, cleaned the house, took care of the boys, and did whatever else was needed to be done. He lost his job as a security guard and started working at a fast food restaurant. I would visit him at his job, but he was distant with me and had an unwanted look on his face. As soon as he started working at this restaurant, his entire appearance began to change. He became very particular about how he looked. Lucious would leave home and arrive at his job on time, but would return home hours after the restaurant had closed. I just watched him and didn't bother to confront him.

Eventually I thought enough was enough and decided to pay an unexpected visit to the restaurant. That particular night, he was to get off early. I showed up at his job thirty minutes before his shift ended and parked down the street. As I sat there waiting, I asked myself repeatedly if I wanted to know the truth or not. Sure enough, I saw my husband coming out of the restaurant with a female co-worker, the two of them wrapped up in each other's arms. They walked together to his car, got in, and drove off. I had finally seen what I did not want to see and went home to sort things out. Lucious did not come home that night, but I wasn't expecting him. I got up the next day and went to work, but called home to ask Jr. if his dad had made it home in time to take Steven to daycare. Of course, he had not.

I told Jr. I was on my way back to the house to pick up Steven because Jr. was babysitting and he needed to go to school. By the time I got home, Lucious had already picked up Steven and were on their way to the daycare. I then called the daycare center and asked the manager to have Steven's father call home. About five minutes passed before Lucious called. I told him in a very stern voice I would like to talk with him and his girlfriend. He replied he did not want to be embarrassed, and he was on his way home to talk. When he arrived, I told him we needed to rearrange our living arrangement to accommodate each other. *"Let marriage be held in honor among all, and let the marriage bed be undefiled, for God will judge the sexually immoral and adulterous"* (**Hebrews 13:4, ESV**).

"What do you mean?" he asked.

I said, "If you're going to stay out all night and not even bother to come home, then it's time for you to move on."

"I'll change, I'll be the father that I should be, and I'll handle my responsibilities," he said. I thought to myself, this man just entertained another woman all night – he must think I am a fool.

"Do you love this woman that you're with?" I asked him.

"I don't love her. She gives me anything I ask for, and I'm weak to the things that she provides," Lucious said. He then went on to promise he would come straight home from work after his shift and take Steven to the daycare center as we agreed. Just as he promised, he did come back about the right time that night, which was also about the time I was getting up to get dressed for my job. As I was getting ready to walk out the door, Lucious asked me for five dollars to buy a company T-shirt. I gave him the money with the understanding he would repay me. He told me to come to his job on Friday to pick up his check and cash it. The rest of the week went well for both of us. However, when I arrived at his job on Friday, one of his co-workers lied and told me he had left early. I asked the manager on duty about Lucious' schedule. He said Lucious was not scheduled to work until that night. Darn it! Lucious deceived me again! I went home and became angrier and angrier every time I thought about Lucious and his deception. I began to pack his clothing in some boxes I had gotten from my job. Later on, that evening, I called his job and asked to speak to him. When Lucious answered the phone, I hung up. I just wanted to know whether he was at work so I could take his clothes to him. I arrived at the restaurant and began to take his clothes from my car and put them in his vehicle. I went to the restaurant and told him not bother to come home for his clothes because they were in his car. I turned around and walked out, not hearing a word he was saying. The following day, he came by to pick up Steven and took him to the daycare center.

Our Marriage Vows

Dearly beloved,
We are gathered here to unite
this man and this woman
in holy matrimony.

By His grace, you have come to this sacred moment. Lucious in taking this woman whom you hold by the hand, do you promise to love and cherish her, honor and keep her, in sickness as in health, in poverty as in wealth, for better or for worse, and be faithful to Carrie so long as you both shall live?
   "I do."
   Carrie in taking this man whom you hold by the hand, do you promise to love and cherish him, to honor and keep him in sickness and in health, in poverty as in wealth, for better, for worse, and be faithful to Lucious so long as you both shall live?
   "I do."

"For the husband is the head of the wife, even as Christ is the head of the church: and he is the saviour of the body. Therefore, as the church is subject into Christ, so let the wives be to their own husbands in everything. Husband love your wives, even as Christ also love the church and gave himself for it" **(Ephesians 5:23-25, KJV).**

After that day, I did not see him for over a week, but I was relieved. I guess I must have spoken too soon. He came by my job and asked if he could come back home. I looked him straight in the eyes and told him to think about what it was he wanted, what he was doing to his family, and to check back with me on Saturday. Lucious' going back and forth and in and out of the house was getting old; he did not know what his role was as head of the house. What I needed was to be loved and nourished like God would have men to love their wives. *"So ought men to love their wives as their own bodies. He that loveth his wife loveth himself"* (**Ephesians 5:28. KJV).**

His parents called that night and said they would be up to visit soon because they wanted to see their son. However, Lucious did not know this. The next day while I was at work, Lucious went by the house. He took my small black and white TV and pawned it. When I got home from work, Jr. came running to me and told me what his father had done. That was it! "Darn it!" I was so upset that I got my boys, rushed to the local hardware store, bought locks, and changed all the locks around the house. Lucious called me that night and said he would bring the TV back home the next night … I guess he wasn't going to bother coming home that night either. He explained he had needed some quick cash and wasn't being paid on time. The next day, while I was at work, Lucious called and said he was going to give me the money and the pawn ticket to get the TV out of the pawn shop.

But I never saw the money neither the ticket. The weekend had arrived, and, much to my surprise, so had his parents. They were expecting to see Lucious, but he did not know they were visiting, so he was not around. Instead, he was over at his girlfriend's house. As his parents were getting settled into our home, I had to think up some excuse for his parents to get Lucious' girlfriend's telephone number. It was getting late. They were growing worried about their son and his whereabouts, and I showed concern too. I told my mother-in-law that if Lucious did not come home soon, we would have to go and look for him. I thought that would be a good time for Lucious to get the shock of his life. By getting everyone together, I wanted to showcase to his parents how their son was living at the time instead of letting God fight my battle. *"Never take your own revenge, beloved, but leave room for the wrath of God, for it is written, 'VENGEANCE IS MINE, I WILL REPAY,' says the Lord"* (**Romans 12:19, NASB).**

"What do you mean?" she asked.

Hmm! I told her I knew where he was and where he spent his nights. The room became silent. You could see his parents' embarrassment and my own. Then the phone rang. It was Lucious. I asked him to hold on for a moment and passed the phone to his mother. I wish I was a fly on the wall to see the expression on his face when his mother greeted him. He must have asked her how long they had been in Dallas because she said they arrived hours ago, and they were shocked to see he was not home at such a late hour. She also told him she called last week and spoke to me about their plans to visit. His mother handed the phone back to me. Lucious said a few choice words while I just smiled and nodded. I interrupted him and asked if he would like me to bring his parents to him on Sinful Street, which was the name of the street where he was living. As he was still yelling, I told him we were on our way and I did not need any directions. I gave the telephone back to his mother. They talked for a couple of more minutes before she hung up.

"Lucious wants you to go and pick him up from his friend's house because his car isn't working, and he'll stay here tonight," she said, with a shameful look on her face and tears forming in her eyes. I became furious and turned around and walked out of the room. No one asked me if he could come back to this house. I stood in my room for a moment and then decided I would not say anything about how I felt. My mother-in-law was only thinking that she would be helping the situation. I calmed down, got my things together, and woke the boys to take his parents to get their son. While driving over to Lucious girlfriend's apartment, I had very little to say to his parents. My going over there would at least give me a chance to see the woman who was destroying our home.

When we arrived at the apartment complex, Lucious was standing outside with a bundle of clothes in his arms as if he had planned on staying awhile. I still did not know the woman's apartment number, just the location. Lucious got into the car and the atmosphere was a bit uncomfortable for everyone. The boys had fallen back asleep. I did not say a word, but the tension was so thick you could cut it with a knife. It was late when we got back home. I told his parents they would sleep in the guest bedroom and told Lucious he would sleep in the boys' room. "Good Night," I said. I took the boys to my bedroom and closed the door. As it turned out, Lucious stayed at the house while his parents were visiting.

He borrowed a friend's car during their visit. The house was uncomfortable for all of us, but we made do. A couple of days before Lucious' parents were to leave, they discussed with him about moving back in with the boys and me. When I got home from work, more of his clothes were found in what used to be our bedroom. I quickly explained to Lucious he would continue to sleep in the boys' room while he was there regardless of what he and his parents talked about the situation between us had not changed.

After his parents left, I asked Lucious for the pawn ticket for the TV and the money he had promised to give me to get it out of the pawnshop. He told me the pawn ticket was in the boys' room in the top right drawer. I walked toward their room, and Lucious walked outside. I looked in the top right drawer and found nothing, but I continued to search and stumbled on several pawn tickets in the bottom right drawer. None of these looked familiar. I waited for Lucious to return from outside, but he had gone. He did not come home for a couple of days, but when he did, I asked him to tell me which one of the pawn tickets was for the TV.

He looked through them and then told me he had some more tickets in his car, but the police had not recovered his vehicle. While I was out on some errands, I went to where his car was and looked all over for the pawn ticket. I ran across several more pawn tickets for things I recognized as my own one was for my heater and the floor fan I had purchased. I returned home and went to the garage to see if any of these things were there. Not finding them, I became angry and went into the house. I met Lucious in the hallway and screamed at him that his butt belonged to me. I walked up to him, got in his face, and yelled, "Someone is going to get a beat down today!" He told me to back off and leave him alone. I was so close to him I could smell the brand of his cigarettes.

Then, I heard my boys cry out to me. Lucious started walking back into the boys' room and sat down on their bed. I turned and went into my bedroom, crying. I was so outraged that I showed a side of me in front of my boys that I never wanted them to see. I could hear Lucious calming the boys. The next day I got up and inventoried my whole house: goods, appliances, anything that could be sold. Items were missing; the pawn tickets I found in his car were items from my home. Nevertheless, he did not take my threats seriously I knew I was going to have to stoop to his level to be taken seriously. At this point, I could take no more and felt like Job when he said, *"Therefore I will not refrain my mouth, I will speak in the anguish of my spirit; I will complain in the bitterness of my soul"* (**Job 7:11, KJV**).

Although he did not have a key to my house, Jr. let him in. After Lucious left, Jr. called me at work and told me his father had taken my radio from my bedroom. I instructed Jr. to call me if Lucious ever came by the house while I was at work, but not to let his father know who he was calling. A couple of hours passed, and Jr. called me again. This time he informed me that his father was back. I told him to hang up, and I would call right back, he should let his dad answer the phone. I called again, and Lucious answered. Acting as if I did not know what was going on, I told him Steven had been asking for him. He said he would pick Steven up from the daycare center. I went on to say that, I noticed some items were missing from my room, and asked if he had taken them.

"Yes," he replied. "I'll return the items soon, though."

I immediately cut him off and said I wanted all of the pawn tickets. I asked if he had to work later on that day.

"No," he said. I told him we need to have a serious talk about this, our marriage, and his urge to pawn things. When I got home that evening, he was not back. I asked Jr. if Lucious had mentioned where he would be.

"He's gone to get your tickets, Mom," Jr. told me. Lucious did not return. The next day, around 9:00 a.m., Lucious called. I had not left for work yet. When I answered, Lucious said he had talked to his mother about our situation.

"That's nice," I said. "We need to get some help, or our marriage is going to end soon," Lucious told me he would try to make things work and went on to say he would be starting a new job on Friday. Also, he needed some money for gas to get back and forth to work. Like a fool, I agreed to give him the money. He came by my job later that day and picked it up. When I got home, he called and asked for more money for a uniform fee. I gave it to him with his word that he would repay me. I asked Lucious if he would pick up Steven from daycare the following evening, and he agreed. The next day, around 4:30 p.m., I called the daycare to see if Steven had been picked up. The receptionist told me Steven was still there. Even though I was scheduled to work beyond my regular hours that day, I told the receptionist I was on my way. Later that evening, Lucious came by the house. When he walked through the door, I just looked at him.

"What?! I just left the daycare, and they told me you had already picked him up," he said.

"It was closed hours ago, Lucious!" I replied. Nevertheless, this was the perfect time to talk with him about our marriage problems.

"Where have you been for over two weeks?" I asked.

"Over at a friend's house," he answered.

"Does this friend have a name?" I asked.

"Look, you know where I've been, so don't ask," he said.

Out of pity, he began to tell me he had been having seizures and that his friend had to take him to the hospital.

"That's nice," I told him as I walked away.

"What do you mean, 'that's nice?'" he asked angrily.

"Well, what do you expect me to say, Lucious?! You have neglected your family, you come and go whenever you feel like it, you are toss-ing it in my face that I am not enough woman for you, so you have to sleep around, and you are stealing from our home. Don't expect me to feel sorry for you." Things got quiet.

"Now, let me show you to the door so that I can go to bed," I said.

"Baby, please let me come back home," he said in a soft voice.

"No!" I quickly responded. "You chose to have someone else, so go on back over there. You can even plan on spending Christmas there because the boys and I won't be here in Dallas."

"How long will you all be gone?" he asked.

"I haven't decided yet," I responded. "So, Merry Christmas and good night."

He said good-bye and walked on out the door. I shut it quickly so that if he looked back, I did not want him to think I was going to change my mind.

Well, time passed. The boys and I had a lovely Thanksgiving, but we did not see Lucious. Christmas was approaching, and we were going to spend it in Miami. Before we left, I asked our neighbors to keep an eye on the house and gave them the number where we could be reached. While in Miami, all I could think about was the house. It dawned on me that it probably was not a good idea to tell Lucious we would be out of town. I did lock everything up, and although he did not have a key, I just kept thinking about how I should not have mentioned we were leaving for the holiday.

Well, I will deal with that when we return to Dallas, I told myself. We had a lovely holiday away. The boys and I needed a change. We left Lucious and the Dallas drama behind in pursuit of a few minutes of peace. *"These things I have spoken to you, that in Me you may have peace. In the world, you will have tribulation, but be of good cheer, I have overcome the world"* (**John 16:33, NKJV**).

Invisible Home Wrecker

By
Avis Lamb Brown

Beware, for I am the most dangerous thing that will wreck your life.

For color, I am not, feelings I have not, but I will love you if you love me.

My reputation is known from coast to coast.

Prejudice! What's that?

I will come to your home, rich or poor.

Once I convince you, your life is not yours anymore.

Smoke me, sniff me, if only for a five-minute high.

I will take you on a trip as your life pass you by.

Attention and love I can give thee.

Oh Boy! I can set your mind free.

I come so cheaply that you can afford to repeat.

I'm the Father's companion when Mother is away,

And the Mother's companion when Father chose not to stay.

Invisible home wrecker, shame am not!

Will mingle with your mind, body, and soul.

I will take over your mind in full control.

That beautiful body now turned wrinkle and old.

That soul you once owned, the life in it, it's now gone.

The invisible home wrecker, I am never alone.

Invisible Home Wrecker is SIN

"The acts of the sinful nature are obvious: sexual immorality, impurity and debauchery; idolatry and witchcraft; hatred, discord, jealousy, fits of rage, selfish ambition, dissensions, factions, and envy; drunkenness, orgies, and the like. I warn you, as I did before, that those who live like this will not inherit the kingdom of God" (**Galatians 5:19-21, NIV**).

Precious Memories
I Am My Grandmother's Granddaughter

I was raised in the 62nd Street projects of Miami, Florida. As a child, my precious grandmother, Carrie, raised me. Carrie was a very religious African American woman mixed with American Indian. Life in Liberty City was exciting and adventurous, but only the strong survived. My day started with my grandmother washing me up and the aroma of grits, eggs, and bacon. My father and his mother raised ten children in a two-unit project home. After breakfast, we always had time to watch TV (Captain Kangaroo was usually on the black and white television). Then it was off to school located in the project neighborhood. I remember so many memories of my elementary school because I was very active. I tried to play the piano, the lessons were free, and then I was a school crossing guard. Later I became the head of the crossing guard.

I remember in math class how I would daydream of places to visit like Hawaii just anywhere else besides Liberty City. In Ms. Holmes' class, I got into a fight with a classmate, and we both were off to the principal's office. When we reported to the office, we both were paddled. I will never forget the pain I experienced. I never fought in school again or anywhere for that matter. Now to survive in the Liberty City project, there were gangs you could join with names such as Big Valley, High Chaparral, and Ponderosa. If we wanted to look at it in color we used a plastic rainbow vertical colored striped sheet on the front of the screen.

Growing up, our family did not have a time clock. My grandmother always depended on her American Indian instinct and wisdom by looking at the sky, the birds, the weather, and changing of the leaves on the tree. Grandmother Carrie was my mentor, and I will always remember the precious memories she gave me. Words from one of her favorite songs verses was "precious Lord take my hand and lead me on." I remember the stories or advice she would give me as she was doing house chores especially washing clothes in the old fashion round washing machine with the clothes wringer on the top and the white round bottom. When grandmother would leave the room, I would play with the clothes wringer. The last time I played with the machine my hand got caught in the wringer. I wasn't punished, but the scar and pain I went through was enough for me to stop.

My grandmother Carrie was a Christian. She loved the Lord with a firm hand and a soft sweet voice. This poem comes to my mind as I reminisce about Grandmother Carrie.

I am my grandmother's granddaughter

By
Avis Lamb Brown

Standing tall, plaits in my head, shoulders broader

Beautiful light-skinned African American woman that she was

Definite a blessing from the heavens above

Precious Lord take my hand, a verse of a song she would sing

Listening to her sweet voice the happiness it would bring

Her southern poise with a touch of pleasingly plump

If you don't behave child, you will get a lump

Yes, ma'am, no ma'am manners, she taught me, only trust in the Lord to lead and guide thee.

Chapter One

What are your thoughts after reading Chapter One?

_____

_____

_____

_____

_____

_____

_____

_____

_____

_____

Have you ever experienced this in your family? If yes, summarize?

_____

_____

_____

_____

_____

_____

_____

_____

_____

_____

Do you know someone who is going through a similar situation?

_____

_____

_____

_____

_____

_____

_____

_____

_____

What can you do to help or be of support to a drug abusers?

_____

_____

_____

_____

_____

_____

_____

_____

_____

My thoughts about Chapter One are supported by the following Scripture as it reveals the way God shows the family, *"who is blind but my servant, and deaf like the messenger I send? Who is blind like the one in covenant with me, blind like the servant of the LORD? You have seen many things, but you pay no attention; your ears are open, but you do not listen. It pleased the Lord for the sake of his righteousness to make his law great and glorious"* **(Isaiah 42:19-21, NIV).**

Who do we blame, if anyone?

_____
_____
_____
_____
_____
_____
_____
_____
_____
_____

Do you believe in God and has He brought you out of life situations that you needed to escape? Share your testimony.

_____
_____
_____
_____
_____
_____
_____
_____
_____
_____

"Brethren, my heart's desire and prayer to God for Israel is that they might be saved" (**Romans 10:1, KJV).**

Heartless Reactions of a Person Hooked on Drugs

WHEN WE RETURNED to Dallas after the New Year, I did a complete walk-through of the house and found everything where it should have been, thank God. We were settling back in when the phone rang. It was Lucious' sister. She was calling because of concern for her brother.

"Have you seen Lucious?" she asked.

"No, I haven't," I responded, "but I have his girlfriend's number if you'd like to check there."

"Yes, I need it," she replied. I gave it to her with a smile in my voice.

"How are you and the boys?" she asked.

"Oh, we're doing fine," I replied. "When you find Lucious, tell him that the loan officer for his car needs a payment."

"I will," she agreed.

"I'm only mentioning this because I co-signed for that car, and it would put me into a financial strain to pay for what is his responsibility."

"Carrie, I know what you're saying. I will try to help in any way I can. Why don't you call my mother and see if she can help you, too?" she offered.

After we hung up, I called Lucious' mother and told her about the situation. She sent two car payments for her son. Afterwards, I thanked her in a letter, explaining Lucious left me with all the bills. Things were a little rough since after returning from a trip.

The following day, Lucious came to my job and asked me for ten dollars. I told him I did not have any money to give him. I reminded Lucious of him telling me the woman he was living with gave him all the things he needed. He should be asking *her* for the money. I also ordered him to stop bothering me for money five dollars here, ten dollars there.

"I am not your bank!" I told him through clenched teeth and then turned around to leave.

Lucious yelled, "You'll suffer without me in your life!"

I turned around to face him and politely replied, "Thank you, sir. Have a nice day." As manager of the store, I had to conduct myself accordingly.

Later that night, long after I had gotten home, the phone rang. It was Lucious' girlfriend.

"You must have a problem, not giving your husband money when he needs it. That's why he's with me and not you." She continued to say she knew how to treat a man.

I responded in a calm voice, "You know, you're right. You are sleeping with my husband, not one of your own." Who did this lady think she was?

I went on to say, "Since you satisfy him sexually, satisfy him monetarily. He should not have any reason to run to me for money because he has you. No, I don't know how to treat him." Then I hung up the phone. I refused to show my anger to a welfare-receiving female, especially over a so-called man, regardless if he was my husband. But as I thought about what she had said, I became furious. Later, on around 4:45 p.m. that evening, I was waiting for Lucious to bring

Steven home; he'd promised to pick up Steven from the daycare center. The hours passed, and I became more and more worried. Jr. came and asked where Steven was, and I told him he was on his way home with his father. The doorbell rang around 10:15 p.m., it was Lucious finally bringing Steven home. I was so angry at Lucious, but glad to see Steven made it home safely. I grabbed Steven and began to undress him, getting him ready for bed. I said nothing to Lucious. I couldn't see straight from anger. As I laid in bed that night, I thought of ways to punish Lucious and his girlfriend. About thirty minutes had passed when the doorbell rang again. When I opened the door, it was Lucious.

"I've got a flat tire, and I need your help," he said. I had a towing service on my credit card, so I called a towing company. An hour passed, but there was no sign of the tow truck. To stay awake while Lucious waited for the tow truck, I went into the kitchen for a snack, and I heard Lucious on the phone talking to his girlfriend. He was explaining the situation and asking her not to be angry. While he continued to beg, I went to the bedroom and picked up the phone.

"Look! I do not appreciate you calling her while in my house." I could hear her laughing.

I then said, "We'll see who has the last laugh." I hung up the phone, stormed back into the front room, and told Lucious to hang up he had to go. I gathered the rest of his belongings, gave them to him, and said, "Get Out!" By that time the tow truck was pulling up. He just stood there saying nothing.

"Anything of yours that is left here, I will take to your apartment. Lucious, you are a sorry excuse for a man abandoning your family and living with a sorry welfare recipient. There is no place in this house for a weak man while I'm trying to raise two boys." When I shut the door after him, I was so furious I could not think straight. All I could think about was revenge, revenge.

I could not sleep so I called my mother. She usually made sense whenever I got angry. Not knowing what time it was, Mother answered the phone and just listened to what I had to say. She could tell I was angry and knew I was having problems in my marriage. I rambled on about the changes Lucious was putting me through and told her about the situation that had just happened. She did not give me advice about what I should or should not do; she did not even say a harsh word against Lucious.

Her only comment to me in a calm voice was to keep the faith. Here I had talked for an hour or so, and she said three words that made everything a little better. I understood what she meant, but in the back of my mind I thought of the satisfaction of getting revenge. At the end of our conversation, she told me to hold my peace and let God fight my battle, and to pray for peace in my home. When she hung up, I felt a little better, so I turned over and fell asleep. As I was drifting off to sleep, I began to listen and hear what my mother was saying about keeping the faith regardless what Lucious was doing to the boys and me. Her words reminded me that it was obvious I needed to begin changing my thoughts. *"Ye have heard that it hath been said, An eye for an eye, and a tooth for a tooth: But I say unto you, That ye resist not evil: but whosoever shall smite thee on thy right cheek, turn to him the other also"* (**Matthew 5:38-39, KJV**).

The next day Lucious called me at home and asked if I would bring the rest of his things to him since his car was not working. This was going to be my last time doing anything for him, and I made this very clear. He asked that I drop his clothes off on the side of the apartment building, and he would be waiting to get them. I took the clothes over and left them on the side of the apartments. As I drove off, I looked in the rearview mirror and saw him taking them away. I started thinking about Lucious having a car and not paying the note, so I decided to steal his car from him. It would not be stealing because I was the co-signer and the one making the payments. Lucious continued to beg for money and take things from the house whenever he visited the boys. These actions helped to make up my mind up to take his car. One night, with the help of a coworker we went to his girlfriend apartment building I got into Lucious' car and drove it off without anyone suspecting a thing. I left the car at my coworker's apartment complex until I could decide what I was going to do. After returning home, I knew the phone would be ringing because of my evasive actions, but he did not call until the next day leaving me to wrestle with my negative thoughts. *"Be not overcome of evil, but overcome evil with good" (**Romans 12:21, KJV**).*

"Carrie, did you take the car?" he asked.

"No!" I responded. "Where is the car, Lucious?! Did you pawn that, too?!" I heard a cough on the phone.

"Who's that?" I said.

"That's my friend."

"Look, Lucious, if you can't talk to me without your friend listening in on the conversation, don't bother to call at all. But since both of you are on the line, let me tell you this: If you two have any problems with anything missing over there, don't call me – call the police." I hung up. Lucious would not dare call the police because of his record.

Around 3:00 p.m., his girlfriend called back. "Carrie, I know that you got his car. "That is why Lucious left you for me; I know how to treat him."

"Let's get a few things straight!" I said. "First of all, you have no business calling me about anything that goes on between my husband and me. Secondly, if I have it or don't have, I pay the car note – not you. Thirdly, I play to win, and if you ever call my job again, I will come over to your apartment and deal with you and Lucious! Try me." I hung up the phone. When I got off work, I went to my girlfriend's apartment and started Lucious' car so the battery would not go dead. I told my friend I would come by at least once a week to start the car and move it to a different spot. I felt good about what I was doing; it was the beginning of a beautiful fight.

Lucious did not call for several weeks, and I did not hear from his girlfriend either. It was nice not having to deal with his infidelity. One day while I was working, I saw Lucious in another car, driving around my company's parking lot. Lucious did not believe I did not have his car. I know he saw my car. He saw me when he looked into the building, but I did not bother to flag him down. I just watched him as he drove off.

The next time I heard from Lucious, he was back in jail I found out it would be for two months. That was another sigh of relief for me. I heard he went into a department store and tried to steal a jam box. When he called me, I asked where he would be staying after being released. He told me his girlfriend said he could not go back to her apartment, so he was coming back to his house. Two months passed, Lucious was out of jail and had moved back into my home. There was nothing I could do because the house was in both of our names - community property. I tried to sell the house before Lucious got out and have his name removed legally as a part owner, but Texas law said something different. So, after he got out, I put locks on all the doors in the house. What an adjustment; to live in a home where all the doors had locks on them. I watched his every move because I did not believe he wanted to make amends at all. He needed to supply his crack habit. I have come to realize what Paul was talking about while I was dealing with a drug-addicted spouse. As a Christian, you have to have faith and believe what the Word of God says *"For we do not wrestle against flesh and blood, but against the rulers, against the authorities, against the cosmic powers over this present darkness, against the spiritual forces of evil in the heavenly places"* (**Ephesians 6:12, ESV).**

I took one day at a time. I knew what I needed to do to get my life back together without Lucious. It was three weeks since Lucious moved back into the house with the boys and me. I didn't mention anything to him about reporting his girlfriend to the welfare office because I knew he was still seeing her. Jr. would tell me his father was calling someone at night when I was asleep.

One day Steven had some candy to sell for school. He brought home a box of twenty. I took some to work and sold them, and Lucious took Steven around the neighborhood to sell the others. Instead of Lucious doing a good deed and helping his son learn to be proud of his efforts, he was casing the community for what he could steal. The following day while I was at work, I received a call that Lucious had been caught trying to break into one of our neighbors' home. What was even worse, it was a police officer's home.

"Well, I guess I have to go and pick up Steven from daycare," I told my boss. I had explained to him that Lucious had been arrested. As I approached the daycare, I saw a couple of police cars. The police officers were talking to Lucious. Steven was looking out from the back seat of one of the patrol carts. My heart started hurting, and I hurried to find a place to park. I could feel the tears forming in my eyes, seeing my baby sitting in the police car. I asked the officers what happened without looking or talking to Lucious because I knew he would only lie again. They explained to me Lucious was trying to break into our neighbor's home, but did not realize the neighbor was watching TV and also watching him attempt to break in. They also informed me that Lucious had crack cocaine in his possession. When Lucious was held at gunpoint by the neighbor who was a police officer, he told the arresting officer to call me. I asked the officers why my child was in the back seat of the patrol car. One officer responded he was letting Steven sit in the patrol car while they talked to his father.

"Mommy! I'm in a police car!" he shouted. I took Steven home, and the officers took Lucious downtown to jail. Minutes after getting settled at home, the phone rang. It was one of the officers checking to see if Steven and I had made it home okay. He knew I was outraged after finding my child in the back of a police car and his father's behavior in front of him. I asked the officer what would happen to Lucious,. He explained Lucious would be in jail for a while because the neighbor was going to press charges (attempted robbery) and possession of drugs. While I continued to talk to the officer, Jr. walked in and could sense something was wrong. After I got off the phone, I explained to Jr. his father had been arrested for breaking into a neighbor's house and that the neighbor lived next door to one of his schoolmates.

"I don't like Daddy. I'm glad he's gone, and I hope he never comes back home," Jr. said in an embarrassed voice. I didn't respond to Jr. because I knew he was going to be teased by the other children when they found out about his father.

Oh, Lord, help me, My heart hurts when I see my child hurting, help me, please! *"Come to me, all who weary and are burdened, and I will give you rest. Take my yoke upon you, and learn from me, for I am gentle and humble in heart, and you will find rest for your souls. For my yoke is easy, and my burden is light"* **(Matthew 11:28-30, NIV).**

All that evening I tried to put things into perspective, starting from when Lucious could have first started using crack and his cheating habits. It was not my fault that Lucious was going through these changes. I may have made a few mistakes, but nothing to drive him to those extremes. Since Lucious was not going to be around, I had to adjust my schedule to accommodate our family. I explained to Jr. that now and then I might need to call on him to help with his brother.

That's when I started depending on Jr., primarily because I was by myself. I was putting so much pressure on Jr. and demanding a lot of his time, but I needed his help. At the time, I did not realize what I was doing by demanding a lot of Jr.'s time, but I needed his help. We did not have any immediate family in the state of Texas. At this time, Jr. was around fifteen years old, and I was considered a single parent with two boys to raise. My work schedule changed from 8:00 a.m. to 4:30 a.m. I would dress Steven and take him to work with me. That would allow Jr. to be home alone to go to school. Sometimes I would forget Steven would be at work with me until he called my name. Then I would take Steven to the daycare during work and pick him up after work during weekdays. If I needed to go back to work as the general manager, he would have to go too. I was leaving Jr. home most of the time, which bothered me, so I tried to make up for it by planning things for the three of us.

A month had passed since Lucious was arrested. He would write, but I never returned any of his letters because I tried to forget him altogether. Lucious had violated everything I believed in a man or partner, and I did not want to have anything else to do with him if I could help it. My days were complete with doing things for the boys and work, and it became so natural that I automatically knew what I had to do each day. I did not have time to think about my problems; I just focused on my responsibilities. Every time I was around the boys, I hid my hurt or pain because I was successful in dealing with problems and difficulties for all of us. I substituted the shame with gifts and outings of their choice. I was going to see to it that they enjoyed their life with me around.

Jr. got a job working weekends at a fast food restaurant. He was excited about starting the job and earning money. Steven went to work with me and slept in my office when I had to work. I was torn between my family and my job. My life was centered around the boys, hoping that someday I would have time for myself. I appreciated my work crew's help with Steven, including my boss. Thinking back and remembering the changes we had to endure, it was a time that could either make you or break you; it is an individual's choice to choose. As the months passed, doing the same routine repeatedly and taking care of the boys; life became more enjoyable. We worked together as a family, free from Lucious' mental abuse. Life without him was a dream come true – we all felt that way. While Lucious was in jail, we managed to keep food in the refrigerator and did not have to lock up our items and rooms. Lucious continued to write to me, but the only time I wrote him was when it concerned something about the house and nothing else.

My in-laws came to visit from the Midwest and planned to visit Lucious at the jailhouse. They had always been around to bail out one of their kids, all of whom were over twenty-five years old. When my in-laws arrived, they called the jail to find out the visitation process. The parole office at the jail told them he would be home within another month, but if they still wanted to visit, they could since they were out-of-towners. They decided not to go. My mother-in-law was happy to hear the news about Lucious being released within a month, but I was not pleased at all when she told me the bad news. Frankly, I wished they could have kept him for several more years.

The month went so fast, and I didn't have time to prepare myself for his arrival. When I heard a knock at the door, I answered it, yes, it was Lucious. I could have dropped dead on the spot. He looked dark and smelly. I told him he was stinking up my house.

"What a welcome," he said. I told him he was at the wrong house expecting a warm and hearty welcome, especially after getting out of jail for the third time. He took a bath and asked how the boys were.

"Fine until about thirty minutes ago."

"I wrote you of my release," he said.

"I wouldn't know because I never read any of your letters, Lucious. Now, where do you plan to stay?"

"Here, in my home with you and the boys."

"Don't do the boys and me any favors, please," I told him. "What about your girlfriend?" He said she moved and changed her telephone number.

"I'm sure you can find other girlfriends to stay with since you had three out there."

He said, "Why are you so interested in where I stay? If you have someone here, I'd leave for a day and come back tomorrow, but he has to go."

I told him, "Don't flatter yourself. If I had someone staying here with me, you would be the one to leave – regardless if this is half your house or not." I went into my bedroom and cried like a baby because Lord only knows I did not want him to stay here anymore. I remembered in the book of Psalms Scripture teaches us about disobedience and the sins of our family member. All you have to do is believe and ask the Lord to help you overcome with these words: "Lord, please help me because I don't understand. *"Cast thy burden upon the Lord, and he shall sustain thee: he shall never suffer the righteous to be moved" (**Psalm 55:22, KJV**).*

When the boys came home, Steven was the only one who was happy to see Lucious, and Jr. did not say anything to his father. I asked Jr. how he felt about seeing Lucious again.

He said, "I hope he doesn't start stealing again from my friends." I told Jr. to take one day at a time just as I was going to do.

All the time Lucious was in jail, I had to send for my nephew from

Miami to stay with us to watch over Steven while Jr. and I were working. My nephew and Steven shared a bedroom, so I had to rearrange the sleeping areas. Steven moved in with Jr. and my nephew, and Lucious slept in Steven's bedroom. Later, Lucious started complaining about sleeping in the same bedroom with my nephew when he was paying the house note. Lucious and my nephew did not get along from day one. I explained that if he had been a man and took care of his family, my nephew would not have been needed when Jr. started working.

"If you could stay out of jail long enough to act like a father, my nephew would not have been sent from my Mothers. You don't like it, too bad – get over it or move out."

About a couple of weeks later I moved my nephew into Jr.'s bedroom and let Lucious have the middle bedroom. It had been six weeks since Lucious got out of jail. I received several telephone calls from my father-in-law saying Lucious told him we were mistreating him, and he did not appreciate my family and me bothering him. At first, I was going to tell his father where they could get off, but I had to remind myself that Lucious had a problem and this was another trick he was using to get one over on his parents. I held my peace and said nothing at the time. Tempers were up, and I was not going to give him any satisfaction now. My in-laws did not fully understand the ways of a drug addict; he would manipulate anyone who came his way.

Lucious finally got a job at a nearby restaurant and needed transportation. He asked his parents for a car. They agreed to give him his third car, the one they used around their hometown. They told him he needed to come and pick up the car from them, so he and his sister went to get it. When he made it to his parent's home, my sister-in-law called and asked me if she could stay with us until she got her place. I told her no without hesitation, and I hung up. Minutes later Lucious called me from his mother's.

"What is your problem, telling my sister that she can't stay with us?! You have your nephew there."

"And he will stay as long as I need him, too," I answered. "Furthermore, I have put up with your disrespect long enough when it comes to your family. Your sister has stayed with us before in the apartments, and one of your best friends stayed with us for a while."

"What are you going to do if she comes and stays against your will?" he threatened.

"Bring her and find out. It's your move." Then I hung up. As I thought about what Lucious was trying to do, I became mad, falling under his manipulation, and called him back.

I told him, "I don't appreciate his attitude when he's with his family. I'll deal with you when you get back to Dallas." About thirty minutes later, I got a call from my mother-in-law. She asked me if her daughter asked to stay until she found an apartment and offered to pay for her stay. I told my mother-in-law she had called, but she did not tell me she would pay for anything. Also, I said to her I did not appreciate Lucious talking to me the way he did, and I had taken enough of his disrespect. She said she was going to stay out of that. I said okay and hung up. Lucious and his sister came back to Dallas, but she did not stay with us. They drove his third car back to Dallas. Little did his parents know that Lucious had a wreck in his second car. He had his parents believing he lost it on the south side of town.

A week after Lucious got the car, it was broken and sitting in the garage. His sister was staying with a friend across town. Lucious continued to lie to his parents about his drug habit. I did not say anything anymore. My heart went out to the parents because they bent over backward to help their kids out in any situation. As the old saying goes, blood is thicker than water.

I finally came to my senses about the living arrangement with Lucious, and I asked myself what in the world I was going to do. At this time, I needed furniture and other household goods before jumping out and moving. I started buying things, saving money, and spending wisely. I wanted revenge, but my conscience would not allow me to hurt him, so my only alternative was to leave. While thinking of leaving Lucious, I also had to think about the boys and what part they played in this move. I decided to put up with his drug addiction long enough to accomplish my goals. I was not being hurt physically, just mentally. I decided to put up with a drug addict and change my lifestyle to achieve my goals before the move.

I said very little to him because he would argue with me about every little thing he thought would get on my nerves. He picked fights with Jr. because he knew how Jr. felt about him. I would get calls at work from Jr. about Lucious accusing him of overeating or ordering him to stop talking on the telephone. I asked Lucious to keep the boys out of our fights. He would reply that he did not like the distance between the two of us, but I told him he'd get over it. The same way I got over all the disrespect and the embarrassment he put us through women, drugs, wrecking cars, and not being able to hold down a job. I told him he needed to get some medical help, or I would help him get some help. I realized I could not deal with Lucious and his addiction by myself; I needed the Lord to strengthen me and turn this situation over to Him. *"Trust in the LORD with all your heart, and do not lean on your own understanding. In all your ways acknowledge Him, and He will make your paths straight"* **(Proverbs 3:5-6, NASB).**

Several years had passed since the beginning of his affairs and drug use. He said he would change and wanted things to be as they once were.

I told him, "It's over. Accept it. I have."

I never let on to Lucious about me buying furniture; he only knew when it arrived at the house. He would ask what I was doing and if he needed to sell his old furniture.

"You can do whatever you like, but what will you sit on when you're watching TV?" I said.

Every time Lucious and I would finish an argument, he would do irritating things like cook food and then leave the house, causing smoke alarms to go off when the food burned. His excuse was always, "I forgot – anyway you're here to take care of it." All I could say was that I was forced to deal with my friend, my lover, and my husband— the crack addict— to accomplish my goals. I developed an attitude to stay alert at all times at home as well as at work. I always expected the worst to happen. I would call home and check on the boys, and my nephew would tell me Lucious wouldn't let them go into his kitchen. I told my nephew to get anything he wanted to eat, and that's why I had prepared dinner for him and the boys. Then I would get a call at work from Lucious, arguing again with my nephew and saying he did not like him staying there.

I told Lucious I did not care how he felt "Please don't bother my nephew, or I will deal with you." My nephew left months later, and Lucious quickly returned to his old routine and left Steven home alone. I prayed to God and started looking for another job so that I could be at home on the weekends and at night with the boys. I found another job working Monday through Friday in an office. *To God be the Glory*. I continued to pray for the peace within my home that I so desperately needed and believed in God's Word that says *"Beareth all things, believeth all things, hopeth all things, endureth all things"* (**1 Corinthians 13:7, KJV).**

The arguments didn't stop when my nephew left. They began with Jr. getting fed up with Lucious's disrespect and embarrassment. He refused to sit back any longer without saying anything to him about his actions toward the family. I understood what Jr. was going through because he had been with me when Lucious started his affairs and drug addiction. I talked to Jr. and told him this fight was between Lucious and me, and I thanked him for his concern. I made him promise me to leave or not say anything to Lucious, if he could, when he tried to provoke him. Jr. questioned me about staying in this abusive relationship and continuing to put up with Lucious' mistreatment toward me.

He stated he did not understand my reasons and he did not like Lucious hurting me. At that time, Jr. stopped calling him Daddy. I told him Daddy is a name a father has to earn, and it was his choice to decide whether he wanted to continue to call him Daddy. At first, Lucious did not take too well with Jr. calling him Lucious. He threatened to hit Jr., but I told Lucious I didn't think it was a good idea, and I would not rest if he ever thought of hurting either of the boys. I would be on him like white on rice. I stayed my distance when arguing with Lucious because I wanted to do something to him so bad.

It was a matter of time before Jr. began to disrespect his dad because of all the hurtful things he had done to the boys and me. Now I had to deal with a disobedient child acting out because of a disrespectful parental action. *"Children, obey your parents in all things, for this is well pleasing unto the Lord"* (**Colossians 3:20, KJV**).

Sometimes when Lucious had just smoked some crack, he would come home and look for something to complain about. Lucious would have such strange looks on his face, moving his tongue like a lizard with a runny nose. I had to nip his arguments in the bud when he had been smoking crack. I remembered a story Lucious shared with Jr. about when he was out on the streets at the crack houses. He told him one night he was smoking crack over at a friend's house. His friend just walked into the house and started beating his wife for no reason. The wife said nothing and just stood there taking the beating. I understood, then what Lucious was trying to do to me when we argued, but I knew he did not have the nerve to get physical with me. Luscious would try to buck up against me, but I stood my ground with caution. Since I moved Steven into my bedroom, Lucious would question why I locked my bedroom door. I just ignored him. Sometimes Steven would knock at my bedroom door, and Lucious would be standing behind him when I opened it as if he was going to do something to me; he would have such a look of hatred on his face.

If I were in the mood to mess with Lucious' mind, I would ask him, "What can I do for you while you're staring?"

His reply was, "I don't like how you treated my son."

I asked him, "Are you sure he's your son?"

Sometimes Lucious would catch me off guard, and I would react how he expected me to respond. It is tough being on guard all the time, trying to overcome a drug addict who lives so close to you. I wasn't going to let this situation break me at all – not with God on my side. I planned on hanging in there until right before I moved.

Lucious would curse me out in front of the boys. I would ask him not to do that, and then Jr. would step toward him in anger. As we argued, Steven would begin to cry. I realized that Lucious was not worth the mental abuse of my kids. At that point, I started ignoring Lucious to keep peace within the family. You know, it made me feel better once I began to ignore the negative comments he always made against me. I talked with my mother, and she told me she was praying for all of us. She also said, my sister (who used crack cocaine and other drugs) had hit her on her forehead with a frying pan. She and my sister had argued all day. My sister went into the kitchen to eat, but instead she took all the food and mixed it together. When my mother approached her, she turned and hit my mother with the frying pan that was sitting on the stove.

My mother said she had ten stitches on her forehead, and she pressed charges against my sister. She told me to be very careful because people on drugs are not their usual selves. I told my mother I was sorry about what my sister had done, but I was glad she shared the incident with me. I had been arguing with Lucious out of anger; she shed some light on my situation about dealing with a drug addict and their tendency to do things without feeling guilt or shame. A drug addict's conscience about what he or she is doing to love ones is never considered. My heart is saddened when I think about those who are captive in a relationship with a drug addict; they are the victims, not the drug addict. They are mentally and physically abused and, in some cases, even death occurs.

Looking at Lucious and being with him from day to day allowed me to see what the doctor meant when he said Lucious had aged ten years or more. His actions and ways were like that of a child. I had to continually look after him and decide if he needed to be watched in everything he did. The boys and I were the victims. I had tried in my limited power to make up for the abuse. I had gathered drug paraphernalia that Lucious used and tried to educate them on the subject of drugs.

Lucious became restless since he was not working. He was caught stealing again and taken to jail. This time he walked into a department store and stole a stereo cassette player. When he called to tell me, I was so happy and looked forward to the peace around the house. He said he took a cassette player because he needed some quick cash. I told him if he needed money, he should keep a job. I went on to say, it was not the first time he ended up in jail, and it probably would not be the last time either – do have a pleasant stay. All the items he stole were pawned, and then off to the crack house he went. Each time Lucious was in jail, I was one step closer to buying the things I needed. It also allowed us a break to get mental relief. When he got out of jail, I was not happy, and neither were the boys. Steven started calling his dad by his first name. Also, he said he hated him and wished he would leave and never come back. I knew it was wrong for the boys to turn against their father, I began to tell Lucious what the Word of God said about his treatment of our sons, *"Fathers, provoke not your children to anger, lest they are discouraged"* (**Colossians 3:21, KJV**).

I'm sure what Steven said affected Lucious, even though he was not in his right mind half the time. It bothered me when Lucious would try to punish Steven. I would react in Steven's defense. We would argue, but I did not care. At that point, I was the only one allowed to punish the boys, considering Lucious' condition. I didn't pay too much attention to Lucious or what he had to say because he had a way of manipulating people. Every time he would talk to me, I had a habit of analyzing every word he said.

I continued to find pawn tickets in Lucious' bedroom and decided not to let Steven stay in the same room any longer. Periodically, I searched his room for drugs and paraphernalia because Steven would sometimes play in there. I am not aware of Steven ever finding any drugs, but Jr. did. Sometimes, I would think of the things my husband had done since he had been on crack for over five years, and I would get so mad at him and myself. However, I decided to hold my peace and let God fight my battle since He was the only One who could.

When I would argue with Lucious, the happy look he had on his face would discourage me. Reality would set in again, and I would have to defend myself in my own home what a violation of privacy. Very seldom would I lock my front and back door, as a thief had been already in my home. Whenever Lucious would leave the house, I expected to hear from the neighbors complaining about him begging for money. When he did not come home for days, I expected the telephone to ring with bad news. I used to think how deserving it would be for him to get caught doing something wrong and end up in jail. I knew not to pray for harm, but Lord, I often thought of it. *"But I say unto you, Love your enemies, bless them that curse you, do good to them that hate you, and pray for them which despitefully use you, and persecute you"* (**Matthew 5:44, KJV).**

Lucious landed another job, and on pay day, I knew not to expect him home for several days. He was paid every week and I looked forward to the peace in my home.

We could never get used to seeing a crack user so closely. His entire appearance was dirty and stinky, and I refused to smell and live with a man who carried himself in that manner. It seemed that when he smoked too much crack, it affected his memory. Sometimes after smoking, he would walk into the house as if he didn't know where he was. When I finally overcame the hatred I had for Lucious and his drug condition, I just looked at him and prayed. There is the old saying, God takes care of babies and fools… and Lucious fit the fool's category. I had to remind myself that he was another lost soul wrapped up in a person who once was so lovable, kind, and caring as my friend, my lover, and my husband.

He would sleep for days at a time, and then eat everything in sight. I stopped putting water jugs in the refrigerator because Lucious would drink out of them instead of using a glass or cup. This was his habit with every beverage in the fridge. We did not trust to eat or drink behind him. As the weeks went by, I still found plastic bags and pipes are used for crack. I saw several burnt brown spots on the carpet in his room. I prayed, "Lord, how much more of this do I have to take?" Please do not leave me alone with this crack-user. I prayed for wisdom, knowledge, and understanding in dealing with his addiction. I also prayed for peace between the boys and me while we lived with him because every day was a challenge. When Lucious would leave I would pray, "Lord, please do not bring him back home – keep him out there." I knew it was wrong to pray for something like that, but you had to have experienced the drug situation to understand my request to the Lord wholeheartedly. I never knew what frame of mind he was in and it was always a surprise when he got home.

When Lucious needed crack and couldn't get it, his eyes would appear glassy as he stared into space. He would become very offensive with me over small issues. I quickly learned to be silent, if necessary, when he was in this condition. I also instructed the boys not to say anything to Lucious unless he spoke first. Whenever he came back to reality, he would tell Jr. his crack stories. I wondered if he realized what he was doing. The more crack stories he shared with Jr., the more his son disliked him. I do not think Lucious understood he was harming his relationship with Jr. *"Now the works of the flesh are manifest, which are these; Adultery, fornication, uncleanness, lasciviousness"* (**Galatians 5:19, KJV).**

He told Jr. a crack story about him and a friend begging for money. They would clear over a hundred dollars a night, depending on the area. He used the family as an excuse to get money, telling people his family members needed help. One time he was over at a friend's house smoking crack with him, and his wife came home from work. She was running late, and his friend just walked up to her, punched her in the face, and said, "Woman, you better have my dinner ready within the hour or I will do something to you, that you wouldn't like."

One morning, he and another crack user were standing on the street corner near a bus stop where a white couple needed directions. The couple needed to go to Blue Hound Bus Station and did not know how to get there. They asked Lucious and his friend for directions and agreed to pay for the information. Lucious and the friend told the couple they would take them to the bus station. They decided to allow both of them into their car. Lucious and his friend got into the couple's car. The man driving let on he had over a hundred dollars on him. Why did he do that? When they got to the bus station downtown, the person they were to pick up wasn't there. So, the couple took Lucious and his friend back to the street corner.

Lucious' friend snatched the driver's wallet and ran from the car. Lucious told the driver he would catch the guy and ran after him as if he were trying to get the wallet from his friend; it was a set-up. Little did the couple know, Lucious and his friend staged the entire incident to snatch the wallet. When they got out of sight of the couple, they split the money between themselves. As I was listening to Jr. tell me these stories, I was convinced Lucious' mind was gone, and he needed help. I couldn't help but think how amazing a drug user will find ways to deceive people so innocent and helpless over drugs. I was so thankful for Jr. sharing this information with me, and I told him I would always be there for him if he had any questions. I did not show any resentment about the stories or Lucious, but I had to show interest for the sake of my boys. Jr. could have kept these stories to himself, or worse, tried to use crack himself.

I had not heard from any of Lucious' girlfriends in a long time, only from his male friends. Lucious would call someone, and minutes later the telephone would ring. If Jr. or I answered the telephone before Lucious, the person calling would say, "Do you still want it?" Jr. or I would answer, "Want what?" Then the guy would ask if Lucious was there, and we would both say, "No," as soon as we realized what Lucious was doing. This particular person would never leave a message or a name. When Lucious had some money, he had the drug dealer call our home. He did not care if I knew it, but he was putting the boys and me in harm's way. Our family needed God to fight this spiritual warfare. *"Put on the whole armour of God that ye may be able to stand against the wiles of the devil. For we wrestle not against flesh and blood, but against principalities, against powers, against the rulers of the darkness of this world, against spiritual wickedness in high places"* (**Ephesians 6:11-12, KJV**).

He would make his call, and then, just minutes later, a car horn would blow in front of the house. Lucious would go outside, then come back into the house and go straight to the bathroom. I hated him for that, and I decided right then I would do something. I noticed from the house window when he made a drug purchase; he always asked for one or two crack rocks. It did not matter to him if I was watching or not. I was numbed at first to what he was doing. This was not the first time it happened, but it was the first time I witnessed his bold move. He had no heart, no self-respect to even try and conceal what he was doing in front of our boys. We all knew what Lucious was doing every time he did it. I resented him having a drug dealer come to my home. I could not believe this was happening in my house. My mind began to wander with fear and concern about our safety. I started to pray because this was something too big for me to handle alone. I talked with Lucious about putting his family and home in danger, I wanted to sell the house, and I wanted out. Thinking only of myself and the boys' safety, I wanted out. He said if we put the house up for sale, I needed to file for a divorce, and he would be rid of me for good. I thanked him for that remark. I told him if he was in such a hurry, he could file for divorce, too. I gave him a lawyer's business card. He became angry and said I was a money-hungry female, only out for myself. However, he wanted to split all the bills down the middle. I just listened, but was still determined to sell the house, regardless of all his comments. He told me to talk to a realtor, and I said, "I already have, and he's on his way."

"That's just like a greedy female," he responded. What he did not know was that I had a realtor waiting for my call. He came over right away and went over the details and instructions about selling the house. We signed the contract I was so hurt because I had wanted my home so badly… but without Lucious in it. However, the law said otherwise. As long as we were husband and wife and both of our names were on the title at the time of purchase, we could not prohibit one another from the home unless it were legally binding. My mind flashed back to when we were signing for the home five years earlier, a time when I was so happy. Now, it was the opposite, and I felt like someone had stepped all over me and there was nothing I could do about it. I never expressed my feelings to anyone at that time because I knew this bitterness and resentment would happen sooner or later. I became more distant and resentful toward Lucious because his presence brought nothing but sadness and danger to the boys and me. I needed words like this Scripture to make it through. *"For his anger endureth but a moment; in his favor is life: weeping may endure for a night, but joy cometh in the morning"* (**Psalm 30:5, KJV**).

When I told the boys about selling our home, Jr. was glad and said it was about time because he hated Lucious and what he was doing to me. It was as if I was losing a child who I had nurtured from birth – losing him to hatred, and all because of a drug-addicted husband and his revenge on me.

Lucious sold everything he owned and was not going to stop until he destroyed everything around him, including his soul. We split all the bills down the middle, or at least that is what he wanted me to think. Whenever we reviewed our budget together, I confronted him about it. He said he was not going to give me anything else, and not to bother him about it again. Based on his continuous actions when it came to money, one of the money Scriptures came to mind that Paul wrote, *"For the love of money is the root of all evil: which while some coveted after, they have erred from the faith, and pierced themselves through with many sorrows"* (**1 Timothy 6:10, KJV**).

"No problem, but I'm going to make sure you eat what you paid for and nothing else. Not to mention, this was your idea from the beginning, and don't forget that." I told him as I walked away I had to remind myself that a drug user is a liar and a cheater and will steal whatever he can get from you. It's as if a person on drugs taking drugs is actually killing themselves; they would be killing the wrong person, because the drugs are actually damaging the human body. Lucious tended to eat everything in sight enough for three people. He is the one who decided to split all the bills down the middle. I told him he took me for granted and I would show him how. One day he walked into the kitchen while the boys and I were eating.

"Where's my dinner? I pay for food in this house!"

I said, "Yes, you sure do, and your share is in the refrigerator it needs to be cooked." I went back to talking with the boys and glanced at Lucious to see the expression on his face. He wanted to say something to me, but I pretended to ignore him. I also stopped washing his clothes. When he told me he needed the car to go and wash his clothes, I told him he could ride along the next time I went to the laundry. He didn't like that at all because he was paying half of my car payment each month. He started complaining about the car. Since he was spending half, he should drive it too. I reminded him of the time I spent over $1800 on the second car that he refused to pay for, and he didn't say another word about my car.

When I went to the grocery store, I bought things I liked and kept them in my bedroom. Lucious questioned me about that, but I told him to mind his own business. Then he wanted to see a receipt, but I never showed it to him. I told him if he had a problem with me going to the grocery store, he needed to go for himself. Lucious was out to make my life a living nightmare, but he was in for a big, rude awakening.

The food was not enough Lucious started snooping through my mail and had the nerve to question me about that, as well. I told him if he thought he already had problems, he would have more if he ever opened my mail. I would become his worst nightmare. I was not taking any more disrespect from him. I had held my peace long enough. His excuse was that I used to open his mail.

"That was before, and this is now, Lucious. We are no longer living as husband and wife. Simply put, this is just an arrangement until the house is sold. So be patient, we will be out of each other's way very soon." From that point on, I tried to be there when I was expecting something important in the mail, but I could not worry all the time about Lucious opening it. I would handle the situation, if necessary.

Lucious became restless again and started asking the neighbors for money. He told them we needed bail money to get Jr. out of jail. He had been doing this for months, but I wasn't aware of it. One of the neighbors said Lucious told him we needed nine dollars to get Jr. out of jail. Another neighbor told me Lucious said he needed twenty dollars and would leave his driver's license until he returned with the money he borrowed. Every time I heard the news from a neighbor, I got a hurt feeling in the bottom of my stomach. It's so hard to believe what a drug addict will do to get a fix or hit. I could not understand some of the things Lucious was doing. He was not aware of the embarrassment he caused the boys and me. The more he begged around the neighborhood, the more the neighbors complained to me because they did not know Lucious was my husband.

It was around Thanksgiving, and Lucious was always trying to take advantage of the neighbors' Thanksgiving spirit. He took medication for his health problems, but would sometimes forget to take his medication which caused him to have seizures. To make me feel sorry for him, he often told me he had had a seizure. I had so little pity for him at this time because he had taken my sorrow for granted. He would use crack before he would take his medication. Now, if he did not have his medication, he would go without it for days as if he did not need it. Sometimes I tried to talk to him about taking his medication correctly so that Steven would never have to see his father having a seizure. I told him he needed to think of Steven and not himself.

"Stop looking for pity from me, Luscious, because I don't have any left to give."

I came home for lunch one afternoon, and he asked if I could drop him off at the hospital. On the way, I asked him when he took his medication last.

"Three days ago." I just started to talk about something else because I was fed up with the way he ignored his health. It was his body and his privilege to treat his body the way he chose to. In the past, I would stay with him at the hospital, but that changed. I dropped him off. If he went in, fine, and if he did not, that was fine too. Lucious was an overgrown child in a man's body and did not have a worry in the world, so you would think he could handle his personal needs. He was always looking for someone to feel sorry for him. I had two boys to deal with, I did not need a third. God tell us to take good care of our bodies and do not pollute them for very good reasons. *"What? Know ye not that your body is the temple of the Holy Ghost which is in you, which ye have of God, and ye are not your own? For ye are bought with a price: therefore glorify God in your body, and in your spirit, which is God's"* (**1 Corinthians 6:19-20, KJV**).

That night Lucious' mother called and asked him how he was doing and what the doctor said about his seizure. I could not believe he called and told his parents about his seizures that manipulating drug addict was at it again. I did not talk with his parents because if I had, I would have told them their son had schemed the entire act of pity and needed someone to feel sorry for him. Again, I am glad I did not try because blood is thicker than water. Every time Lucious went to the hospital, I never expected him to come home because he stayed out for days. If I did not see Lucious for two days, I was not surprised. Also, whenever he came back, he always had a look about him you could not help but notice and say, "Hmmm." He reminded me of a walking human skeleton with a layer of skin, wearing an Afro.

Lucious had been gone for an entire weekend when Steven was sick. I had to nurture him back to health so he could return to school. I came home from work on Monday and as I walked in the house there was a foul odor coming from the bedroom where Lucious was sleeping. He would sleep for days at a time. I would check his breathing to make sure he was not dead. The boys told me that when Lucious had come into the house, he first walked in the front door and walked around to the back. The entire time he walked around, he was licking his lips with his tongue out like a lizard. The boys just watched with concern, and I told them to stay out of his way when he was like that and not to say nothing to him. Lucious would not say anything to the boys, or anyone for that matter. He would come into the house and go to sleep. The boys and I would not know the state of mind Lucious was in when he was on crack. I continued to pray for God to keep His arms of protection around our house and everyone in it. *"For God hath not given us the spirit of fear; but of power, and of love, and of a sound mind"* (**2 Timothy 1:7, KJV**).

White as Snow

By
Avis Lamb Brown

Welcome, Welcome
White powdered snow
You came into my life, and I can't let go
My soul is lost for less than a penny of the cost
The pride had died, and I continued to lie
My wife, my son, Lord, help me to overcome
Mr. Snow, Mr. Rock
You came into my life without a knock
You entered into my mind of your own time
My sense of thought is hard for me to unwind
Shameful, Shameful, why I can't be
Of my choosing how I accepted thee
America the beautiful that welcomed the
Powdered snow
Freedom to be distributed
Everywhere you want to go
In the land of opportunities, guaranteed to please
Stands in control with every lock and key
Welcome every citizen and set their minds free,
From sea to sea
Thank you, Lord, for continuing to
Bless my family from me

"Submit yourselves therefore to God. Resist the devil, and he will flee from you" (**James 4:7, KJV).**

Chapter Two

What are your thoughts after reading Chapter Two?

_____

_____

_____

_____

_____

_____

_____

_____

_____

_____

Have you ever experienced dealing with an addict in your family?

_____

_____

_____

_____

_____

_____

_____

_____

_____

_____

Do you know someone who is going through a similar situation?

_____

_____

_____

_____

_____

_____

_____

_____
_____
_____

What can you do to help or how can you be of support to an abuser?

_____
_____
_____
_____
_____
_____
_____
_____
_____

My thoughts about Chapter Two - God is showing the family how to, *"Gently instruct those who oppose the truth. Perhaps God will change those people's hearts, and they will learn the truth. Then they will come to their senses and escape from the devil's trap. For they have been held captive by him to do whatever he wants"* (**2 Timothy 2:25-26, NLT**).

Who do we blame? The drug addict, the drug dealer, or is there anyone?

_____
_____
_____
_____
_____
_____
_____
_____
_____

Do you believe in God and has He brought you out of life situations that held you captive? Share your testimony.

_____

_____

_____

_____

_____

_____

_____

_____

_____

_____

"Peace I leave with you, my peace I give unto you: not as the world giveth, give I unto you. Let not your heart be troubled, neither let it be afraid" (**John 14:27, KJV**).

Senseless Acts of a Drug User

IT WAS ANOTHER year, the weather was beautiful and cold, and we were all at home. One evening, there was a knock at the door from some visitors at Lucious' church. Steven answered the door and ran to tell Lucious they were here. Lucious was not in the mood to have company, especially not church visitors, so he asked Steven to say he was sick. I allowed the visitors to go into his room after I spoke with them because he was not ill, just sick in the head. I refused to let Lucious use the boys or me for his lies. The church members did not bother Lucious and said they would come back at another time. When Lucious finally woke up and came back to reality, he made a phone call. Of course it was the same person who came when he had drug money.

Minutes later a yellow car pulled up in front of the house. Lucious went outside and did whatever he does and headed back into the house. I had walked outside just as the car was driving off. He acted as if nothing had happened and said nothing to me. I thought my presence might scare off the drug dealer, so he might be more careful about coming to my house in the future. What I could not understand is as long as I did not say anything to Lucious about the company he kept, he would continue to put his family and me in danger. I decided to take a stand against Lucious and his disrespect toward the boys and me in our home. I never brought up the subject of him and his friend in the yellow car, but my actions said it all very loud. However, if it is not one thing, it is another. The neighbors began to complain more and more about Lucious and his habit of borrowing money. He brought more shame and embarrassing moments to our home. Although I grew fearful for the boys and me, the Word of God says, " Even *though I walk through the valley of the shadow of death I will fear no evil, for you are with me; your rod and your staff, they comfort me" (**Psalm 23:4, ESV).**

Lucious finally admitted he was not working; he would leave in the morning as if he was going to work. He had no choice but to tell me because I would come home for lunch and he would be there. I told Lucious whatever he chose to do with his time was strictly up to him, but not to include me.

That same night Lucious left the house Steven and I were watching television. A few minutes later, I heard an unfamiliar voice. He had the habit of telling salespeople who came by the house to talk to his wife – "She's the one with the money." He continued this until I had the chance to embarrass him in front of a salesman. I said, "I'm sorry, sir, my brother has a mental problem, and he misleads people by calling me his wife. I'm his sister." I just walked into my bedroom and started laughing so hard I cried it was a good feeling. I never not had that problem with him after the last incident. I realized the only way I could get some results when dealing with Lucious and his addictive behavior was to meet him in his craziness and enjoy doing it.

So, I walked back into the living room and found a strange person who Lucious had allowed into our home to use the telephone. I walked into the kitchen, and the stranger approached me. He asked me how I was doing and said he was sorry my son was in jail. I said, "I beg your pardon, sir, but my son is not in jail. He is at work, and he has never been in jail before. Where did you get that information from?" He said, "From your husband." I told the person, who was a neighbor from two streets over, I was sorry my husband bothered him, but he had a habit of lying and fantasizing if he did not take his medication. The look Lucious gave me; I bet he could have rolled me into a crack pipe and smoked me up! As the neighbor was leaving, he asked if he could see me outside. I followed him outside and told him it would be to his advantage to call the police if he ever saw Lucious around his home. The neighbor said they would take matters into their own hands when it came to a person who would lie about his kid. He did not appreciate Lucious bothering his family at home. Whenever I heard the terrible news about Lucious, it did not hurt me anymore because I knew what I had to do, I had to take a stand and show him I could act just as he did and be very convincing – beating the devil at his own game. He started this game, and I planned to finish it with pleasure. Lord, I know vengeance is Yours, so help me to understand it.

When I walked into the house, the boys and I just laughed because they said Lucious left out of the garage door very angry. I told the boys we were going to take our house back from the crack addict, reassuring them Lucious was not going to embarrass us anymore without a laugh. The three of us were going to stand together. After that night, I was not enduring anymore nonsense from Lucious. He would soon see. Lucious did not come home that night, which was nice. It was too much heat for him. We were going to turn the embarrassment he intended for us, back onto him. If he stepped out of line again and pulled another stunt again in our home, his selfish acts belonged to me. I was not going to be embarrassed anymore by Lucious. If he brought another stranger into the house, he would have a verbal fight on his hands. I always tried to be the one who was calm and keep peace in the family, but now he created a monster. I would not yield to this temptation; I began to sing songs of praises trying to keep my focus on God's Word that says, *"The Lord is my light and my salvation, whom shall I fear? The Lord is the stronghold of my life of whom shall I be afraid?"* (**Psalm 27:1, ESV**).

The following night we had a visit from another neighbor this time a white couple who was concerned about Jr., of course. Lucious told them we needed some money to get his stepson out of jail. He was standing behind me when I told them how sorry I was my husband bothered them. I explained he had a problem 'lying' if he didn't take his medication. "He's all right, just needs rest." I developed a strong will to stand against Lucious and his drug addiction and was prepared for anything he would dish out. The more we had unwelcome visitors at the house, the more Lucious saw I was no longer going to take his disrespect and embarrassments. The next day he had a visit from the person in the yellow Cadillac; Lucious did his usual routine: went to the car, went to the bathroom, minutes later he flushed the toilet, and then off into dreamland. A week passed, and I did not hear any complaints from the neighbors about Lucious begging for money. I knew he was up to no good. Whenever the telephone would ring, I expected the worst.

Then it happened again with a neighbor I knew for over four years. He said Lucious came to his house while his mother was alone and asked to borrow five dollars. The neighbor said he wanted Lucious to pay his mother back since she was on a fixed income. The reason he was telling me was that if he saw Lucious again, he would take care of him. The neighbor's mother had seen Lucious and he asked for her five dollars, but he acted as if he did not know what she was talking about. He went on to say he had never seen her before. By that time, the other neighbors saw Lucious standing there, and they told him he had also borrowed money from them.

However, Lucious continued to lie about ever borrowing money from any of them. They called the police, and the cops told Lucious he better not be seen in this neighborhood again, especially begging from them. The neighbor asked me if I wanted him to take care of Lucious for me. I told him no, but thanks anyway. I did tell my neighbor I was sorry about his mother being caught in the middle of this mess. As he walked away, he told me, "I better not see him in my neighborhood, because I don't appreciate him calling my mother a liar." I wanted to tell Lucious about the conversation with the neigh-bors, concerned for him about the lies he had told for months. I told him the neighbors all decided to handle the matter themselves. He said he was not going to think about what they were saying, and they were not going to do anything to him, anyway. I was learning how to turn Lucious' shameful actions over to God because the Word of God says, *"Cast thy burden on the Lord, and he shall sustain thee; he shall never suffer the righteous to be moved"* **(Psalm 55:22, KJV).**

Things were happening so fast surrounding Lucious' habit of bor-rowing money in the neighborhood. Sometimes I would sit down and try to understand what in the world was going on and why. I would call and talk to my mother, and she would try to console me. It didn't help; it seemed like I needed something more than talk. I listened to other people tell me about their situations, but no one would ever tell me how to handle the heartaches, shame, and embarrassment that comes with it. During the past twelve months, I did not fully understand the hurt. I am the type of person who can handle what-ever comes my way. However, how can you challenge or handle a drug addict who has no feelings or shame? I thought I could find my answers by listening to others, but the more I listened to others, the worse it seemed. I wanted an instant answer. I continued to pray to the Lord for peace, knowing He was working situations out because HIS Word says, *"Be anxious for nothing, but in everything, by prayer and supplication with thanksgiving let your requests be made known to God"* (**Philippians 4:6, NASB).**

I began to participate more in church activities and felt comfort-able, but I dreaded when I had to go home. As time went on and the more I went to church, I started listening to what the preacher said. I noticed the message was directed at me. It was as if I told the preach-er to speak on that subject. After the sermon, I briefly talked to my pastor about my problem. His response was to pray and turn it over to the Lord and leave it there. At that time, I could only think about how I could have spared myself some of the grief and pain if only I had turned it over to the Lord sooner. I began to pray to the Lord and thank Him whether it was good or bad news. I learned to turn it over to Him and started to see results over a period of time just by leaving my problems and not trying to assist the Lord. After I realized I could overcome my problem and win without even fighting, it felt good and comforting at the same time. *"And we know that all things work together for good to those who love God, to those who are called according to His purpose"* (**Romans 8:28, NKJV**).

Lucious continued to pull his impossible stunts with the neighborhood, but he saw a change in my actions. I tried to talk to Lucious, this time out of concern for his health. I told him he needed to consider professional help, or he was going to lose his life or his family. After that conversation, Lucious' entire attitude changed toward me. He stopped taking baths and quit cleaning his bedroom and picking up after himself. It came to the point I threatened to bathe him fully dressed in the bed, while he slept. His excuse was he felt just fine, and it was not bothering him. When Lucious got some money, I offered to take him to the store and demanded he purchased his hygiene items. After he took a bath, he would leave the house for days and return looking and smelling so bad I refused to allow him to sit on anything until he took another bath. I resented Lucious for exposing the boys and me to this kind of treatment in and out of the house while dealing with his addiction. However, the more I prayed to God the stronger I became. *"Be strong and of a good courage, fear not, nor be afraid of them: for the Lord thy God, he it is that doth go with thee; he will not fail thee, nor forsake thee"* (**Deuteronomy 31:6, KJV**).

I learned early on if I took Lucious to the department store to buy clothes, he would return them with or without the receipt, or sell them to get the money. Over the weekends, there would be no Lucious sometimes until Sunday. Once, to my surprise, he came home early. I was surprised, and then there was a knock at the door. It was the church members to pick him up for church service; they all left together. I was surprised, but I knew something was up. When Lucious returned from church, I was cooking dinner. He came into the house and used the telephone. Minutes later, the phone rang again. Lucious answered it and hung up saying only, "Yeah." Later, the person in the yellow car drove up and Lucious went out to meet him. Then, the car drove off with Lucious in it, maybe because he saw me looking at them from the kitchen window. Minutes later, Lucious came back into the house from the garage and off to the bathroom he went.

He had money from his church members and bought some crack with what they had given him. My heart was sad for the church members who were being used to supply his crack habit; He had used God's people to get drug money. They tried nothing but to help Lucious, and he played on their compassion. What a troubled soul. I know Lucious manipulated the church folk, fed them a story, and they believed him. It is sad because they seemed sincere in their concern for Lucious. They prayed here at the house for Lucious and gave him Bible literature, showing a genuine interest in him. Sometimes he would attend weekly meetings at night with them they were trying to convert him without getting professional help. During the whole ordeal with crack, he always said he did not need professional help, and he could quit by himself. Then I knew he had a problem and was too weak to seek professional help. We all need the Lord to guide and lead us especially when a family member is on drugs. I decided to help Lucious get some help, but first I sought God's guidance according to His Word that says, *"But seek ye first the kingdom of God, and his righteousness, and all these things shall be added unto you"* **(Matthew 6:33, KJV).**

One Sunday Steven went to the church with Lucious. He was afraid because they were the only black people there at church and the members were sometimes staring at them. However, Steven knew Lucious had attended this church before. They were on their way back home from church, and Lucious stopped by the side of the road to urinated. Steven said he was so embarrassed while he waited. He begged me not to let him ever go back to church with his daddy or anywhere for that matter. I told him it would not happen again. To get his mind off earlier events, we went to the movies and out to eat. I felt terrible, but tried not to show it. At this point in our marriage, I learned to expect anything to happen when Lucious was around, and I made sure the boys were not involved.

When we got home from the movies, I received a call from my mother. I shared this story with her, and she started to laugh saying, "What's wrong with him?" Then my mother said she would continue to pray for my family and me, but I must keep the faith. When Jr. got home from work, I told him what happened. We continued to laugh about Lucious' behavior and reminisced about his other drug situations. It was nice to see a change in our attitude, the laughter that was long overdue. When Lucious came into the house, we all looked at him and began to laugh. He didn't know what was going on.

Lucious was still out of work, of course. Things around the house needed to be fixed, and the grass needed to be cut. I could not afford to leave my yard equipment out because Lucious would sell it at the local pawnshop. He tried to get Jr. to give him access to the yard equipment, but Jr. never would because he knew what he would do with it. The only time Lucious ever touched the yard equipment was when I decided to work out in the yard. He sold so many things from the house it is hard to remember. Now, I was accustomed to living with all my salable items being locked up. He has never said he was ever sorry for all the things he did to the boys and me by stealing and selling things from the house. I felt like I was a prisoner in my own home having to lock up stuff from my husband, the head of the house. I knew the Lord would change our situation one daybecause He said in His Word *"This poor man cried, and the Lord heard him and saved him out of all his troubles"* (**Psalm 34:6, ESV).**

I just accepted the fact Lucious had become a useless person who society had to take care of for the rest of his life unless he got some help. I had to replace all my pots and pans because while we were asleep, he would cook and burn the pots so badly I could not clean them. Sometimes the smoke alarm would go off, and he would say he forgot he was cooking. His mind was all smoked up from using crack cocaine. I started putting food in my bedroom so the boys and I would have something to eat. If I did not, I would have to buy extra food and going over my budget without Lucious' help. He did not care if the boys ate or not; he just worried about himself. When they were at home alone with him, while I was at work, Lucious would not cook for the boys. This action on Lucious' part was so disheartening to me. A father, a man of the house, would not feed his children; I knew the Lord would change this situation one day. His Word says, *"Then shall the righteous answer him, saying Lord, when saw we thee and hungred, and fed thee? Or thirsty, and gave thee drink?"* **(Matthew 25:37, KJV).**

Lucious pretended to be looking for a job and showed up at my place of employment. When I saw him, I could have melted into the carpet. He looked so bad as if he just woke up from sleeping under a bridge for a couple of days. I ignored him but asked what he was doing while he was there. He saw I was ignoring him, so he finally left. But when he got home, I told him not to come to my job ever again looking like a bum. Also, I told him he embarrassed me. But when I thought I could handle any of Lucious' embarrassing moments he would hit me with something else.

Then I asked Lucious, "By the way, what did you want?"

"Why are you keeping food in your bedroom from me?" he asked.

"What's it to you what I do in my bedroom?"

He said, "I don't think it's fair to keep food from me."

I replied, "Listen to me, you're a drug addict. Life is not fair to those who look out only for themselves. You are wasting your life away and only out for yourself!" I knew I could not let him get me angry because that is what he wanted. Lucious had so much time to think of things to argue about and tried his best to break me down fat chance. After I continued to seek God's help, I began to get myself together and not let Lucious get to me. I paid half of everything around the house, and I did not owe him an explanation of any kind.

Later that day a package arrived, and I was glad Lucious was not at the house to receive it. The box was delivered to the neighbor's house next door. When I got home from work, there was a note telling me where my delivery was left. I went to the neighbor's home to get the package. She said another neighbor called her and asked if she knew us. She said she knew the boys and me, but only knew the husband until recently. The other neighbor said they were afraid of Lucious and would take care of him if he ever comes to their home again. She said they called the police and were told they could not do anything until he came on their property. I didn't know what to say, but I was sorry for what Lucious had done. If he came to her home again, she could call the police. She felt relieved. When I got home, I said to myself, darn it. I can't go and visit anyone in the neighborhood without being embarrassed about Lucious' actions. Nevertheless, I held my head up; this would be over soon, and I needed to be strong for the boys. I figured if they saw me holding out, then they would too. I know I am a good mother and it was my friend, my lover, my husband who was not worth the ground he walks on. My heart felt as if it had been stabbed so many times and in a different spot each time, with the news of Lucious' embarrassing moments. Through it all, I pressed on and remembered God does not put anything on you that you cannot handle. Reading the Word of God brought hope and peace to my mind and heart. *"There hath no temptation taken you but such as is common to man: but God is faithful, who will not suffer you to be tempted above that ye are able; but will with the temptation also make a way to escape, that ye may be able to bear it"* (**1 Corinthians 10:13, KJV).**

Sometimes I would ask the Lord a question: "Lord, how much more do I have to endure with this crack addict? Please don't leave me." When I felt low and thought of what was happening in my life all around me, I remembered God loves me as his child. Every time I read the Scripture above, it would calm my mental state of mind. Jesus was burdened with pain and humiliation and bearing His cross daily will signify our trials and hardships.

I decided to call and talk with my mother-in-law about the neighbors and their complaints about Lucious begging them for money. She told me she did not want to hear about Lucious and his condition and hung up the phone. At first, I was a bit upset with her for not being interested in what I had to say about her son. As I thought about being a mother we want our sons and daughters to be the best they can be. It was hard to imagine how she had been feeling about Lucious and his entire drug condition because I had been wrapped up in my own feelings. Later, I would get a chance to tell her I was sorry and that I did share her concern about her son. Weeks passed, and I hadn't heard from my in-laws, so I decided to call to keep the line of communication open. We talked about everything else except Lucious.

During the conversation, I could hear the hurt in my mother-in-law's voice. I told her I appreciated her and the things she and Pop had done throughout our marriage. I looked forward to visiting her during the holidays. I knew my in-laws would always be around for their son. Blood is thicker than water. One time my mother-in-law questioned my putting up with Lucious and complaining about his comings and goings. I told her when I married Lucious, it was for better or worse, and that I took those vows very seriously. I said to her, "When I have had enough, I will leave when I am ready, and not by someone else's decision. Our marriage covenant has been broken by the Lord's covenant, the Lord because of Lucious's adultery and cracks addiction; I know the Lord will deliver us out of an ordeal he said it in his Word for us to remember. *"Let marriage be kept honorable in every way, and the marriage bed undefiled. For God will judge those who commit sexual sins, especially those who commit adultery"* **(Hebrews 13:4, ISV).**

It was Christmas time, and we were expected to go to Lucious' hometown. Our plans changed due to Lucious and his drug habit. I called my mother-in-law to tell her we were not coming because Lucious was not coming with us as a family. I told her I refused to leave my home unattended with him alone. I was concerned about the boys' Christmas presents she had for them, but she said she would send the Christmas presents to them. It all worked out for the family, considering the state that Lucious was in at that time.

Tears of Joy and Pain

By
Avis Lamb Brown

Tears are universal, we all can share

Life is unique when we show affection; we show we care

God controls the flow of our tears, as we cry in pairs

We label our tears for love, tears of joy, tears of sadness,

However, tears are just tears

Tears are also known as weeping

T in tear shows our tenderness

E in tears shows our emotions

A in tears shows our affection

R in tears shows rejoicing

S in tears shows sorrow

Depending on the situation, we may not want to live for tomorrow

Do not give up; hang in there, a change will come along

As you grow in your Faith with a praise report and song

"They that sow in tears shall reap in joy" (**Psalm 126:5, KJV).**

Chapter Three

What are your thoughts after reading Chapter Three?

_____

_____

_____

_____

_____

_____

_____

_____

_____

_____

Have you ever experienced this in your family?

_____

_____

_____

_____

_____

_____

_____

_____

_____

_____

Do you know someone who is going through a similar situation?

_____

_____

_____

_____

_____

_____

_____

_____
_____
_____

What can you do to help or how can you be of support to an abuser?

_____
_____
_____
_____
_____
_____
_____
_____
_____
_____

My thoughts about Chapter Three - God is showing the family, _"who shall separate us from the love of Christ? Shall trouble or hardship or persecution or famine or nakedness or danger or sword? As it is written: "For your sake we face death all day long; we are considered as sheep to be slaughtered"_ (**Romans 8:35-36, NIV**).

Who do we blame, if anyone?

_____
_____
_____
_____
_____
_____
_____
_____
_____
_____

Do you believe in God and has He brought you out of life situations you needed to escape? Share your testimony.

_____

_____

_____

_____

_____

_____

_____

_____

_____

_____

"Therefore do not be anxious, saying, 'What shall we eat?' or 'What shall we drink?' or 'What shall we wear?' For the Gentiles seek after all these things, and your heavenly Father knows that you need them all. But seek first the kingdom of God and his righteousness, and all these things will be added to you. "Therefore do not be anxious about tomorrow, for tomorrow will be anxious for itself. Sufficient for the day is its own trouble" (**Matthew 6:31-34, NKJV).**

Dangerous Actions Between the Family and Drug Dealer

THE MONTH FOLLOWING Christmas, Lucious pawned Steven's remote-control car that he and his sister had purchased. We decided to get it out of the local pawnshop. Lucious had not bought the boys anything for the past two years, except the remote-control car for Steven. They had not looked for any gifts from him for birthdays, Christmas, etc. However, they didn't buy him anything either. As for myself, I had to get used to not giving Lucious a Christmas gift during the holiday due to the pain he had caused us throughout the year. Knowing his track record, all he would do with the present was take it to the pawnshop. It was a habit I had to break from blessing each other with a gift. During the holiday's Lucious would frequently come to the house and try to argue with Jr. and me about not getting him anything for Christmas, but we just ignored him.

When the time was right, I decided to talk openly with Steven about his father's drug condition. This was very difficult with much hesitation to tell him his father suffered from a medical condition and drug abuse problem. Some of the issues we were having were because of his daddy's illegal drug use. Jr. said, "Mom, just let me handle him because I am very frustrated about the way he treated you. I told him to allow me to control it, as it was my battle. That's when I assured him we would be okay, and I would treat the matter very delicately during this ordeal. After talking openly about Lucious' drug problem, we began to grow closer as a partial family, even though I knew Steven did not quite understand. Months passed before Lucious got out of prison, as always, his presence was not wanted in the house.

I continued to pray while going through these trials and tribulations and hoping that it would not have a permanent effect on the boys. There were days Jr. need to let off some steam about Lucious' habits and actions in the house. I told him to come to me if he needed to talk about Lucious' drug habit and release his frustration. He agreed.

One day my mother-in-law called to check on her son. This time I let her talk; I did not mention a word about Lucious' ongoing drug use. She told me she was happy Lucious had joined a church and was singing in the choir. As she continued with what she believed about Lucious, I could not go along with the lie I was hearing from her any longer. I just listened and waited until she finished. Then I told her, "I'm sorry, I wasn't aware Lucious had joined a church and the choir. You need to talk to Lucious. Now, I will not lie for Lucious, and I will always tell you the truth about your son if you ask me." I was furious with Lucious for not telling his mother the truth about joining the church. When Lucious did not share the truth of him not going to church with his parents, I refuse to get between him and his parents. It's baffling how well drug addicts lie to make themselves look innocent. I waited for him to come home to tell him his mother called and that she would call back later that night.

That same night someone blew their horn for Lucious. Then the telephone rang at the same time – it was his mother again. I told my mother-in-law Lucious had just left in the yellow car with a friend, and I did not expect him to return that night. She asked me to have him call her even if he had to call collect. She informed me she discussed his condition with his dad, and they wanted him to come home and get some professional help. Again, my mother-in-law comes to the rescue. I told Lucious about his mother's call when he returned home the next day. To my dismay, he continued to use drugs and sold anything of value in the house to buy them. It was extremely overwhelming how he would curse me out with no remorse the woman he had once loved.

Another weekend with the rock star, and he was on the prowl again based on his appearance and action. Conversation with Lucious was minimal as always, so I decided to clean the house and wash clothes. I informed him he would need to wash his own clothes since everything was split down the middle between us. While cleaning the house, I stopped to wash several loads in the washing machine and then went back to cleaning areas in the house. Several minutes later I went back to check on the load of clothes and as I walked toward the laundry room, Lucious assumed I was going to wash his clothes.

He shouted out loudly, "Don't bother with my clothes or any of my things!"

I told him in a low tone, "Don't worry, my spouse, I will not touch any of your things. And another thing for that matter, I haven't had the desire to be with you for over five years, and I don't see it happening soon." I forgot Jr. was in the bathroom during this argument. He came out and asked what was going on. I told him Lucious, and I were discussing his cleaning duties. I reassured Jr. there was no reason to be alarmed because Lucious was just having a relapse from his relationship days with me. I continued to clean and said nothing to Lucious. That night, Jr. came to my bedroom, while Steven was asleep and shared another story with me about Lucious.

A few nights before the police stopped Lucious because he was out begging for money again. They arrested Lucious and made him lay on the ground face down. They also asked for identification and asked if he was the person begging for money in the area. Of course, he lied. They asked him if he lived in that area. He said he did and was walking to the neighborhood store. They told him to get up and go home while they followed him. If he did not tell the truth, they would take him straight to jail. Lucious called the police's bluff and made a telephone call, and told whoever was on the other end he wanted to meet at the usual place.

Jr. said, "Mom, my friends, and I were listening to the entire conversation." This was so embarrassing to hear from my son and his friends.

"Did you say anything to Lucious?" I asked.

"No," Jr. answered.

"Good, that was a smart move. How do you feel about what's going on?" I opened Pandoras box with that question. He said he did not understand why I was staying with Lucious and putting up with his crack habit.

"In time, Jr., there will be a change. Just be patient with me." The next day, I went to church. I looked forward to going to church because it gave me the strength, inner-peace and the determination I needed. Now and then, I often thought about Lucious and his crack habit and remembered he was once my friend, my lover, and my husband. By falling into the hand of the devil, crack had taken him from me. It seemed as though, I was losing: it was not worth it to try to fight for someone who was not willing to fight for themselves. My days had been bearable living in the same house with a crack-head because I overcame a great deal of anger. However, Lucious and I somehow agreed during one of our discussions to put the house up for sale; I contacted a realtor with all the necessary information.

The weekend was over, I was back to work. When I got off from work and went home, I had a message waiting on the answering machine. The information was for Lucious, so I went to his bedroom. A foul odor hit my nose as I opened the bedroom door. I told him I refused to live in the same house with him. "You might not care about your body odor, but I do! As long as we're under the same roof, you will clean your dead-smelling body!"

He got up and got dressed without taking a bath. While dressing himself, he told me he wished I would take me and my smart mouth where he could not see me anymore.

"In time, my dear, in time," I told him. We were trying to desperately sell the house. We soon got a call from the realtor to say he had someone interested in the house and would bring them by around noon the next day. I told him I would make sure the house was clean, and everyone would be away. The following day when I got home from work, Lucious had been home all day and the house was a mess. I knew what he was trying to do. He had been at it since the house went up for sale. I managed to clean the house with the boys' help, and we went out for dinner while the realtor was showing the house.

The next day I worked late. My nephew, John, came to visit us in Dallas, and he stayed with Steven. He overheard Lucious talking on the telephone, telling someone he could sell something Wednesdays and Thursdays. My nephew put two and two together. He had seen Lucious at a neighborhood convenience store and never thought anything about it. Now he knew what Lucious was doing, selling drugs. One of my nephew's friends saw someone he knew buying something from Lucious. It was the drugs Lucious was selling. I told him to watch himself when Lucious was around and to tell me if he said anything out of the ordinary.

John and I grew up in the Liberty City area in Miami and were exposed to the drug and alcohol environment. Reliving my upbringing in Miami from the projects on 62nd street to a home in Liberty City is what I tried to change when I got married and moved to Dallas. Regardless of what city life's trials and tribulations brought, Paul teaches us in the Word of God to "*Humble yourselves, therefore, under the might hand of God so that at the proper time he may exalt you, casting all your anxieties on him, because he cares for you. Be sober-minded; be watchful. Your adversary the devil prowls around like a roaring lion, seeking someone to devour. Resist him, firm in your faith, knowing that the same kinds of suffering are being experienced by your brotherhood throughout the world. And after you have suffered a little while, the God of all grace, who has called you to his* eternal glory in Christ, will himself restore, confirm strengthen, and establish you" *(1 Peter 5:6-10, ESV). Amen!*

My sister-in-law called every other day to gossip about Lucious. I just listened to what she had to say. She wanted to turn Lucious into his parole officer because she felt he needed to get some professional help. I told her about the neighbors' complaints regarding him begging for money and how he said Jr. was in jail and we needed nine or ten dollars to get him out. Also, how they were tired of him begging and were ready to take matters into their own hands because the police said there was nothing they could do. She asked me what he said about the neighbors' complaints. I told her he said they would not do anything to him, so he continued to beg for money. I had not seen Lucious for a few days. She kept going on about turning her brother in to his parole officer, and I told her to be careful. "He may be your blood brother, but he is someone else when he's on drugs."

The following morning at about 5:28 a.m., I heard the front door open. It was Lucious coming from an all-nighter looking as stoned as ever. Although Jr. would soon be getting up for work, it was the front door opening that woke me. I went into the kitchen and noticed the oven was on; Lucious must have forgotten about it. Since I was off from work that day, I decided to clean out the garage. It was then when I noticed Steven's bike was gone.

Later that day I asked Steven, "Where's your bike?"

He answered, "Daddy asked to borrow it for a couple of days." I was so angry with myself for leaving the bike unlocked and for believing Lucious was not going to sell it again. I waited until Lucious came home and asked for the pawn ticket for Steven's bike. He said he would pay to get it out and needed the money to buy Steven something else.

"Don't say another word, because I really can't listen to any more of your lies." I found out he got $18 for pawning Steven's bike, which was just enough to get a couple of rocks (crack). Lucious had bought the bike for Steven with his parents' help about eight months earlier. I decided to talk to the boys about Lucious and his drug habits again and a particular situation when he managed to manipulate Steven. I should have known better than to give Steven the key to his bike, but I learned from my mistake. I took the key from Steven and put it in my bedroom explaining to Steven he would need to wait until I was home to ride his bike. He would need Jr. to unlock it for him when I was not at home. I told Jr. I was afraid Steven might lose the only key to his bike. At the same time, this may have helped Steven realize his daddy had a problem with drugs. Nevertheless, he was so innocent and still believed everything his daddy told him. I hated to do that to my son, but it hurts every time Lucious would sell his toys I learned to watch what I said around the boys, especially Steven because I realized the words of a parent with a crack-addicted spouse could be like the following Scripture. *"Your tongue plots destruction, like a sharp razor, you worker of deceit"* (**Psalm 52:2, ESV**).

Another year was about to end, and Christmas was coming, a time to be joyous again. The boys and I went to church, and we were to be reminded what Christmas is all about - love. While I was cooking dinner, I was in the Christmas spirit. As I watched Channel 21 on the television, the program had another message of love. It hit home with me. Living with Lucious while he was on drugs had been very, very difficult and painful. Just remembering some of the things he did, none of it made any sense. He would start arguments for no reason and try to watch a show on my TV especially when the boys wanted to watch their program in the living room. I had to remove the cable out of the house because we never got a chance to see it as long as he was at home all day. Anytime the boys watched TV, he would make remarks and just kept nagging them until they did not want to be around him. *"I have told you these things, so that in me you may have peace. In this world, you will have trouble. But take heart! I have overcome the world"* (**John 16:33, NIV**).

Finally, I was able to accept his presence until I accomplished my goals and was ready to move on. I began to realize I must come to terms with the anger and bitterness I felt toward Lucious. My lifestyle changed, but this was something I had to do. One thing I could not get used to having a man who was not working and him not being the man I once knew. He was as low as low can get, taking drugs and ruining his life while we watched.

As time went on and I met more people who shared my experience, I learned what others had to say. I had an agitated friend who called and wanted to know how I was doing with Lucious and his drug habit. She said her mother moved in with her because her sister, who was living with her mother, started taking drugs. She continued by saying that her mother left her furniture at home for a week until she found a place of her own, but when she went back home, her daughter had sold her furniture. Her mother cried on the telephone and told her to call the police because she was getting ready to fight her child for selling her furniture. My friend said she felt very sorry for her mother because she took her sister and her kids into her home when they were homeless. While she was sharing her story about her sister and mother, I remembered my mother telling me about one of my sisters who was on some unknown drug. She hit my mother in the head with a cooking pan during one of her cravings. I always thank God for His arms of protection around the boys and me. He continued to shield us from any physical harm while dealing with Lucious addiction. *"No weapon that is formed against thee shall prosper, and every tongue that shall rise against thee in judgment thou shalt condemn. This is the heritage of the servants of the LORD, and their righteousness is of me, saith the LORD"* **(Isaiah 54:17, KJV).**

The family atmosphere is pleasant now. It took a whole lot of praying and discipline to overcome the drug conditions in my home. While in our house, we gave up many privileges because Lucious fought against me and took it out on the boys every chance he got. When the boys were out of school on different school breaks, he would watch them and not let them be boys and go outside. He was just in the way.

WOW! Every time I looked around it was getting close to Christmas again, it seems like every time I look around another year was about to end, and I still didn't have Lucious' help. It seems with all the issues in our home I lose track of times and months. I got home from another day of working and had a message on the answering machine; it was Lucious' sister. She was trying to convince Lucious to go home and get some professional help for his drug habit. They also talked about getting in touch with his probation officer to transfer him to his hometown. Lucious returned his sisters call that evening. His sister asked him about pawning Steven's bike at the local pawn shop and asked when he was going to get it back. After I heard the message, I went into the living room where Lucious was watching TV. I asked him if he was considering going to get professional help; I would send his clothing and let him know if the house sold.

However, he decided not to go. Whenever, I tried to show some concern or try to get rid of him, he refused to leave. Lucious was in no hurry to get help because he could continue to beg the neighbors for money to get his next fix. I got a message on my answering machine; it was Lucious' sister, again. Lucious was asking her for money to get his driver's license back. Moreover, he had borrowed money from a neighbor and had to repay the money to get his license back. He borrowed $15 toward his license, and his sister agreed to give him the money. His excuse this time was so he could get Steven's bike out of the local pawnshop. I knew Lucious had not changed, but where did he get his ideas? I continued to pray for Lucious and his deceptions toward me, as well as his crack addicted attitudes, because I knew he was in trouble with God and man. *"There are six things that the Lord hates, seven that are an abomination to him: haughty eyes, a lying tongue, and hands that shed innocent blood, a heart that devises wicked plans, feet that make haste to run to evil, a false witness who breathes out lies, and one who sows discord among brothers"* **(Proverbs 6:16-19, ESV).**

The following day, Steven had one of his neighborhood friends over at the house for a visit. While on his way home, Lucious approached the boy and asked him where he lived and if he had some money. I saw Lucious talking to the boy from a distance while driving down the street in the opposite direction. I immediately turned my car around and headed toward the boy and Lucious. When I asked the boy what he and Lucious talked about, he said Lucious wanted to know where he lived and if he had some money. I could not believe it, but it sounded like Lucious. I went to the little boy's home with him, met his mother, and told her what Lucious did. I told her if Lucious came around their house uninvited to please call the police. As I was leaving, I felt so hurt and ashamed of having to confront strangers and talk like that about my husband, but thought I had to do this regardless of my feelings.

One day when Steven and I got home from a shopping mall, my sister-in-law was over for a visit in the kitchen. She came over to give Lucious the money to get his driver's license back. She needed change for her money, but I did not have any change to give her. Instead I gave her directions to the nearest grocery store. Lucious and his sister left together. When they returned, my sister-in-law gave me the money to get Steven's bike out of the local pawnshop. I wondered when they would see Lucious for who he was: a drug addict. I wished they would not bail him out every time he did something wrong.

The weather had changed with the season about nine degrees. When I took Jr. to work I decided to pick up Steven's bike from the local pawnshop on my way back home. I hated going into the pawn shops, but it was for my baby boy Steven. The following day I bought the boys a movie and video: because it was cold outside, and they would be confined to the house all day. Steven decided he wanted to go outside, so he asked his dad if he could. As he was leaving, I asked him where he was going.

"Outside," he answered.

"No, it's too cold. Stay in the house," I told him. Then Lucious came to my bedroom and said he told Steven he could go outside. I told Lucious I was not aware he permitted Steven to go outside and, "Sorry to bother you with our family problems," I said.

He said, "What do you mean?"

"I sometimes forget you're a father to him," I answered.

"If you keep bothering me, you will regret it! I hate you!" he yelled. Then he decided to come into the bedroom where I was and continued to argue. He told me I could move out if I did not like where I was staying. He also stated he did not appreciate me saying things like that in front of his son.

"I told him, I don't like you are smoking crack and begging my neighbors for money either, but I'll get over it and so will you what we each dislike."

Lucious told me if I continued to get in his way about his son, he would hurt me.

I responded, "Well, I do have you well-insured, dear." I did not say much to Lucious, but I watched my back after his remarks because I did not trust him. This was not the first time he made threats toward the family we would defend ourselves, if needed. I have learned it is senseless to argue with a drug addict because they are not the same person; it is the drugs they are using them. Instead, I seek God's guidance because *"God is our refuge and strength, a very present help in trouble"* (**Psalm 46:1, ESV).**

It had been over three weeks since I heard from the neighbors about Lucious begging for money, but I had a feeling someone would soon complain. While home for the holidays and I got a message on the answering machine from Lucious' parole officer. He asked for Lucious, and Lucious answered the telephone. He acted as if he was someone else, and he told his parole officer Lucious was not working. Now, keep in mind this was Lucious talking to his parole officer. The parole officer told Lucious to tell Lucious he needed to get into the office because he had not reported in that month. Lucious told his parole officer that he would tell Lucious that he called. I was listening to all of this, but I was full of the Christmas spirit and refused to let Lucious and his drug habit interfere with my holiday cheer. I had not put out the Christmas toys yet because Lucious was home during the day for most of the time. I did not want to go to the local pawnshop around Christmas time to get them out. I never believed he would ever stop pawning our things. It was just a part of his life, and I did not believe he was planning to change anytime soon.

As the year passed, Christmas was the most memorable time and the weather was perfect. The boys were playing in the living room and enjoying their gifts, especially Steven. He got a video game and I knew he would play it about twenty times between then and next year. I cooked a big dinner for the family hoping it would last about four days if I was lucky. Lucious decided to strike again and took Steven's remote-control car set and sold it the day after Christmas when Steven stopped playing with it. What a dog! I could not believe he would do something so low during that time of the year. I forgot I was dealing with a heartless crack addict. Lucious said he needed the money and, anyway he bought it in the first place and could do as he pleased. My in-laws called and wished us a Merry Christmas. I told my mother-in-law it would have been a lovely Christmas if Lucious had not sold Steven's remote-control car set he and his sister bought him. Then my mother-in-law said Lucious did not buy Steven's the remote-control car set - my sister-in-law did. Lucious lied again! There was no doubt he continued to convince me he needed some professional help.

I returned to work, and the boys were still out of school for the next couple of days. After work, while walking toward the front of the house I noticed a bag. I looked inside and found some of my ceramic Christmas ornaments; I could not figure out what they were doing outside the front door. I went into the house and asked the boys if they were using the ornaments. They said they did not know anything about it. I did not have to look any further because I knew it was Lucious' doing. The boys said he had been in and out all day. After that I did a check throughout the house to see if anything else was out of place. Everything was accounted for, thank God. I did not bother the boys with Lucious and his problem. We managed to ignore him throughout the year while he was still going strong with the crack.

I received a telephone call the next day from Lucious. He wanted to borrow some money, but I told him I did not have any money to lend him. When I got home, Jr. told me he saw Lucious at the shopping center blood bank. He said Lucious sold his blood and sometimes plasma to buy crack. I told Jr. not to say anything to him. Jr. said he did not and would always hide when he saw him because he was either begging for money or embarrassing him in front of his friends. Jr. also said this was not the first time he had seen him near the blood bank, but he never thought anything of it before.

The boys and I went out for dinner and talked about Lucious and his drug habit with a sense of humor. While eating, John told me Lucious had a visitor earlier that morning, it was the guy in the yellow car. Lucious bought several joints from him, but Lucious didn't see John when he got the joints. When Lucious saw him, he went into the bathroom and smoked them. It did not matter who was in the house. John said Lucious did not care about smoking the joints because he opened the bathroom door while they were in the house. My nephew said he left a note letting me know he did not like how Lucious was mistreating him when I was not around. After realizing he left his house key, John went back into the house, walked toward the bathroom. He noticed Lucious lying on the bathroom floor.

Lucious was shaking, choking, and having a seizure. John had previously seen my baby sister Tee having seizures. He noticed Lucious was shaking and choking, but he just stood and watched him. Afterwards, Lucious got up and went into his bedroom and fell asleep. As a precaution, John kept an eye on him while he was asleep. I asked my nephew why he did not call me at work. He said he did not want to bother me, because he knew what to do. By now it was close to the time for me to get off from work. *To God be the Glory* for keeping Lucious while he was using both illegal drugs and prescription drugs; however, he was destroying his body daily. *"If anyone destroys God's temple, God will destroy him. For God's temple is holy, and you are that temple" (**1 Corinthians 3:17, ESV**).*

One day my mother-in-law called, asking about Lucious. I told her he was not home and still smoked crack in the house in front of the boys while I was at work. I explained that I asked him not to, and I had given explicit instructions to the boys to call the police if he did it again. My mother-in-law said to do what I had to do and tell Lucious she needed to talk to him and call her when he got home. I needed to talk to him. Unfortunately, Lucious never came back that night. By the tone of my mother-in-law's voice, I could tell she did not want to hear what I had to say about calling the police on him. However, this issue had to be addressed whether she liked it or not.

The following day, Lucious came home. I told him his mother wanted him to call her. Instead, she called back the next night and while they were talking, the answering machine was recording their conversation. I don't think he realized what was happening. My mother-in-law asked him how he was doing, and he said okay. She asked him if he got in touch with his parole officer and talked to him about coming home to get professional help. He said that his parole officer was supposed to get back with him about leaving Dallas and having his parole transferred. She told Lucious to tell her when he contacted him so she could make plans. His family never ceased to amaze me. They always fed into his lying stories, especially his mother!

Lucious never once talked to his parole officer. He never intended to leave his comfort zone or stop smoking crack. The parole officer called every month pleading with him about coming in for his monthly meetings. When Lucious got off the telephone, I asked him why he found it necessary to keep lying and be dishonest with his mother. "It's none of your business. Stay out of my way," he answered. The weekend came Steven and Lucious were supposed to go to the movies. I disapproved when Steven went anywhere with him. I dropped them both off at the movie theater and told them to call me when it was over. A couple of hours later, I received a telephone call from Lucious, telling me to come and pick them up from the movies. When I picked them up, Steven looked sleepy. We returned home, and I put him to bed. When Steven woke up, I asked him how the movie was.

"Momma, we didn't go to the movies. We went to a house where people were smoking glass, cigarettes and crying and coughing," he told me.

"How did you get there?" I asked.

"We walked to the store where you shop for food, Momma," he said.

"Are you sure, Steven?"

"Yes, Momma," he answered.

"Well, then, how did you get back to the movies?"

"We got a ride. Daddy told me not to tell you that we didn't go to the movie, so don't tell him I told you, okay?"

If Lucious had been in sight, I would have ended up in jail for beating the daylights out of him. He must have known Steven would tell me about not going to the movie, he was looking forward to seeing. I continued to question Steven about what happened at the house where his dad took him and what was going on at the house.

He said, "Daddy told me to wait on the stairs while he went into the house. Then I looked inside for him, and when I walked in, I saw a lot of smoke. I started choking, so I went back outside. When I went back to the house, I saw Daddy smoking a glass cigarette. So then, I just played outside until he was done.

When Daddy finished, and I asked him if we were going back to the movies now, he said, 'Yes.' However, Momma, when we got back to the theater, Daddy told me he did not have enough money for the movies, and not to say anything to you. He promised to take me some other time.

Not in this lifetime, I thought to myself. I just sat for a moment, entirely in shock, thinking of all the bad things that could have happened to Steven while he was at a crack house. From that day forward, I did not allow Lucious to take Steven anywhere with him. My heart ached so bad after finding out where Lucious took Steven I just sat in silence and cried to the Lord for help, in keeping my boys safe, I knew He would, He said it in His Word: *"But the Lord is faithful. He will establish you and guard you against the evil one"* (**2 Thessalonians 3:3, ESV**).

When My Heart Says It's Over

By
Avis Lamb Brown

You feel relieved from bitter and hurt in the heart

As you look at each other as you part

Looks, not words are said

When you know the relationship is dead

I guess with you, dealing with crack my best wasn't good enough

As you go through life allowing your crack addiction ego into
thinking you are tough

The blood flows through your heart just like mind

As you get older after the crack addiction,
I pray your heart will become kind

Our heavenly Father controls our heart and feelings

Misleading, deception, embarrassing and shame toward each other
makes the relationship not worth dealing

"He heals the brokenhearted and binds up their wounds"
(**Psalm 147:3, NKJV**).

Chapter Four

What are your thoughts after reading Chapter Four?

_____

_____

_____

_____

_____

_____

_____

_____

_____

_____

Have you ever experienced this in your family?

_____

_____

_____

_____

_____

_____

_____

_____

_____

_____

Do you know someone who is going through a similar situation?

_____

_____

_____

_____

_____

_____

_____

_____
_____
_____

What can you do to help or how can you be of support to an abuser?

_____
_____
_____
_____
_____
_____
_____
_____
_____
_____

My thoughts about Chapter Four - God is showing the family *"but let all who take refuge in you rejoice; let them sing joyful praises forever. Spread your protection over them, that all who love your name may be filled with joy"* (**Psalm 5:11, NLT**).

Whom do we blame, if anyone?

_____
_____
_____
_____
_____
_____
_____
_____
_____
_____

Do you believe in God and has he brought you out of life situations you needed to escape? Share your testimony.

_____

_____

_____

_____

_____

_____

_____

_____

_____

_____

"Trust in the Lord with all your heart, and do not lean on your own understanding. In all your ways acknowledge him, and he shall direct thy paths" (**Proverbs 3:5-6, KJV**).

MISTAKES, MI-STAKES

By
Avis Lamb Brown

Spelling and meaning are the same

Often misused for personal gain

Where did the word come from?

Human-made

We use it like a tongue blade

Humans make mistakes, mi-stakes, God does not

Continue to live, continue to make mistakes, don't stop

With God's help, we learn to accept

Mistakes, Mi-stakes in such a graceful way

Mistakes are a part of our life; we learn to accept them day by day

"If we confess our sins, he is faithful and just to forgive us our sins and to cleanse us from all unrighteousness" (**1 John 1:9, KJV**).

Helpless Reactions From a Person on Drugs

IT WAS A new year. Lucious' birthday came around and we did not celebrate it at all, it was just another day. My mother called to wish him a Happy Birthday, and we talked about how the family was dealing with his drug habit. I told my mother about Lucious taking Steven to a crack house when he was supposed to have taken him to the movies. She told me my sister Ann, who was on crack and using other drugs, had gotten pregnant at a crack house. Ann was living at the crack house with her crack boyfriend, but she gave the baby up for adoption. She asked me how I was doing, and I told her I was excellent, now that I had put things into perspective about living with Lucious. After that incident with Steven being in a crack house, I realized Lucious would go to any lengths to get a rock (crack cocaine), even if it meant exposing his son to that environment.

My mother always left me with a kind word about praying, and that is one reason I was able to have some peace of mind and move on. I began to get my house in order by working and caring for the boys. Seeking revenge was far from my mind because "Vengeance is Mine said the Lord," not mine to seek. First, I had to compose myself and let nothing Lucious had done, upset me unless it was a life-threatening matter to the boys or me. Secondly, I tried to understand and work with Lucious and his drug habit, giving him the benefit of the doubt. Lastly, as long as I helped him, he would continue to use me and anyone who tried to help him. He was a complete user of drugs and people. Sometimes he would try and use parts of our marriage vows to convince me it was for better or worse. I would listen to that crackhead person and say, "Lord, help him." *"The Lord is my Shepherd; I shall not want"* (**Psalm 23:1, KJV**).

The Lord only helps those who help themselves. I had not heard any complaints from the neighbors about his begging. However, I knew he was still doing wrong because it was not in his blood and mind to do the right thing. After all, he needed crack. So, I tried not to let him bring his drug addict friends into my home until I moved elsewhere. I kept hoping God would one day change his heart. *"But they that wait upon the LORD shall renew their strength; they shall mount up with wings as eagles; they shall run, and not be weary; and they shall walk, and not faint"* (**Isaiah 40:31, KJV**).

I continued to watch him just in case he tried to steal my things. I noticed he took my garden tools from the garage, so I replaced them and locked them up. Lucious had developed his only means of survival, and that was selling his blood or plasma out of his body. He continued with his old dirty tricks such as coming near my job to take care of some business at the Life Skills office that were located across the street. However, I said nothing to him, and just observed him and his actions. When he was leaving the office, I noticed him picking up a cigarette from the ashtray out in the lobby area. Lucious was once my friend, my lover, my husband, but it was hard to believe he had stooped so low to get caught up in the smoking crack crowd. Lucious' actions showed a sign of weakness when it came to hanging with the group, and I was afraid for him and our family. *"The Lord is my light and my salvation; whom shall I fear? The Lord is the strength of my* *life; of whom shall I be afraid?" (**Psalm 27:1, KJV**).*

Eventually, I filed for child support against Lucious and was waiting to hear from them. The letter finally went to one of his girlfriend's apartment office as well as our house. Lucious was not a happy camper when he received his copy. In fact, we had some unpleasant words with each other. A husband brings a sense of responsibility, and Lucious had not supported his family since he got out of jail. He was moving in and out of the home and into the home of other women. I did not care at that point.

Now, Lucious began to take an interest in Steven's well-being because of the child support papers he received. He got some money, and I did not say anything about him getting Steven something for school. Lucious asked me to take him to the mall to get Steven a shorts outfit; this would be the first piece of clothing he purchased that year for Steven. That year Lucious' mother sent him a winter coat and I hoped she did not pay very much for it; the one she sent before he sold and lied to her that it was lost. It was winter now, and Steven managed to lose his winter coat again. It happened every winter since he had been in elementary school. Of course, I was the one who had to buy him another one. When Lucious heard Steven had lost his winter coat, he asked me why I had not told him.

"Because I thought you pawned it," I answered. He did not respond to the comment.

I needed to get away for some time to myself, so I arranged for Steven to go to my sister-in-law's house while I attended my 10-year college reunion. I enjoyed the time away and did a lot of thinking about my family and future. If I stayed with Lucious in his present condition, things could get worse. It was hard to let go of something so beautiful and come to terms with leaving my home, comfort zone, and my feelings. Going away for the weekend was something I needed to refresh myself and gain strength. *" Be strong and courageous. Do not fear or be in dread of them, for it is the LORD your God who goes with you. He will not leave you or forsake you" (**Deuteronomy 31:6, ESV**).*

Sometimes while working in the yard or just talking to the neighbors, I often thought about how Lucious had embarrassed the boys and me during this crack cocaine ordeal. Each day presented thoughts about leaving Lucious, or have him put away. But when? It had to be soon. Up to that point, the boys and I had avoided any physical harm by him.

School was going to be out soon, and my mother had planned to visit me for two weeks. I was looking forward to her visit, but not while Lucious was up to his old tricks. My mother and I talked about her visit, she still insisted on coming to Dallas. I did some extra cleaning because I expected her to try and clean for me. Although Lucious knew she was coming, he continued to do what he did best - smoke crack and stay out all night … a good time for him to go to jail.

Drugs had been a part of my family while living in Liberty City, Miami. My mother knew how to handle drug addicts like Lucious After she arrived, the boys went with me to pick her up from the airport. On the way back to the house from the airport, we stopped and got something to eat and talked about the family. I told her I was glad she had come to visit and looked forward to our quality time together. I asked her not to allow Lucious' dirty appearance to bother her, and she asked me how I was holding up. Personally, most of the time I did not understand which way to go and some days I found myself just sitting still and alone. *"Trust in the LORD with all thine heart, and lean not unto thine own understanding"* (**Proverbs 3:5, ESV).**

"Most of the time, I'm just fine, but this so-called marriage is old, and a change need to happen soon," I replied. Every time we talked about Lucious, she would start up with my sister Ann and how she was receiving drug treatments. One thing was different, though, because Ann admitted she had a drug problem and wanted to get professional help. Lucious was enjoying living his life in the fast lane. My mother always had something kind to say and reminded me not to forget the Lord. This was always nice to hear. A Word about the Lord sounded like sweet music to me, especially when my mother quoted the words of King Solomon: *"Pleasant words are as a honeycomb,* *sweet to the soul, and health to the bones" (**Proverbs 16:24, KJV**).*

When we arrived at the house, Lucious was there, trying to act as if we were one big, happy family. He and my mother talked, and she immediately told me it was not anything but the devil himself in the house with me. I told her I already knew it and was why I needed to leave as soon as I could. I was not off from work during the two weeks my mother was visiting, but I wanted her to relax and enjoy her stay anyway. She and Lucious were often at the home together during the day. She said she noticed he had some of the same ways that Ann had when she was using crack. I told her not to leave her money where he could get it, but she assured me, "Don't worry, I've lived with a drug addict before." She said I was sorry that she and I had to relive bad memories during her vacation.

Whenever we went sightseeing or hung out together, I never considered involving Lucious. I did not want anyone coming up to me on the street asking about my husband and saying he owed money to a lot of people. I did not want to take my chances with Lucious and his drug habits.

I tried to make my mother's stay as pleasant as possible. We went to Sunday school and attended services at the church where I was a member. One particular Sunday, I was bringing a sub-topic of the Sunday school lesson to the Sunday school class. I felt like a little girl showing off in front of my mother. In fact, that was the first time my mother had ever seen me speak to a group; it felt good. I missed having my family around especially during my marriage problems.

I insisted my mother sleep in my bedroom during her visit; however, she preferred sleeping in the living room on the sofa bed. My mother complained about Lucious staying up all night while she was trying to sleep. He was not very considerate at all.

"You should have asked him to turn off the TV while you were trying to sleep," I told her.

"No, this is still his house," she replied. I told her I would talk to him about his actions, while being careful to keep my cool and not argue.

My mother-in-law called and I overheard my mother talking to her. My mother said she was delighted to visit me and needed the rest, but she missed being at home. I knew she did not want to be at my home in between Lucious and me. When my mother left to go back home I was sad to see her go. The boys and I took her and my nephew to the airport. She told me to be careful because Lucious was full of the devil and would try anything. I assured her I would take care of myself, and the next time she visited I would not be living with him. After her visit, I was convinced it was time for a change. I needed to flee from this toxic marriage as soon as possible. There is *"a time to weep, and a time to laugh; a time to mourn, and a time to dance. A time to cast away stones, and a time to gather stones together; a time to embrace, and a time to refrain from embracing; A time to get, and a time to lose; a time to keep, and a time to cast away; A time to rend, and a time to sew; a time to keep silence, and a time to speak; A time to love, and a time to hate; a time of war, and a time of peace"* **(Ecclesiastes 3:4-8, KJV).**

How long can my luck hold out while living with a drug addict who was once my friend, my lover, and my husband? When I got home from taking my mother and nephew to the airport, I found Lucious waiting to talk to me.

"I didn't appreciate you leaving me out of everything when your mother was here," he said.

"Your feeling does not faze me one bit, and I am not concerned about what you appreciate or don't appreciate. Furthermore, if you were even half a man and not a drug addict, you would get some professional help and then maybe, just maybe, I would look at you differently. Until then, back off!"

"Well, two can play this game," he replied. "When my parents come to see me, we're not going to let you come along anywhere we go."

"Hey, count this player out, Lucious, and that would be fine with me." You can continued to talk about my mother and the way you were ignored for the last two weeks I don't care. I refused to argue with him and just walked away, but not with my back turned. Jr. came into the house and noticed Lucious was arguing with me. He came to my bedroom to ask what was going on. I explained Lucious didn't like how I treated him while my mother was visiting, and was voicing his opinion to himself. "Just ignore him, Jr."

My mother called to let me know she and my nephew had a safe trip home, but I did not tell her Lucious waited until she left to argue with me. It was enough he hung around during her visit. I decided to work in the front yard that day to get some exercise. Soon enough, Lucious came outside and started shouting at me about not being the wife that I should be. I said nothing to him and after listening to him complaining for ten minutes, I went back into the house to get away from him. He followed me back into the house still yelling, so I knew he wanted to fight. I refused to give him the satisfaction and went to my bedroom and locked the door. First, I knew I needed to calm down because if he kept arguing, one of us would end up in jail. I could hear him calling me all types of names and rehashing arguments from the past. Minutes later, the yelling stopped. Lucious had gone into his bedroom to go to sleep.

I calmly went to the kitchen and got a knife. I went into the bathroom and sprinkled water on my face. I then walked into his bedroom and stood over him while he was lying in bed. Several drops of water from my face fell onto him while he slept. He opened his eyes and was shocked to see me standing over him with a kitchen knife in my hand. He laid there helpless. When I knew I had gotten his attention, I walked out of the bedroom backward without saying a word and locked myself in my bedroom. Later that evening, I found a large stick that was similar to a two by four. The next day, I placed it on Lucious' pillow he did not say a word to me about the stick or the knife. Those two incidents were not enough for me though. I needed to get his undivided attention one more time to make sure my message was received: I would not put up with his arguments any longer.

I put together my mother's old-fashioned recipe she had poured on my abusive, alcoholic father to escape another beating. The recipe called for a broken light bulb, syrup of your choice, and lye – all boiling in a pot on the stove, waiting to be used when the time was right. If Lucious saw this, I knew he would remember what my mother and I told him about my abusive father. Whenever he drank alcohol, he had a habit of beating my mother. She had five kids at the time, all under the age of twelve. My mother got tired of my father's physical abuse, so she decided to beat him at his own game. Every time my father would call and tell my mother he would be home late, she knew he was drinking and with another woman, so she expected a beating when he got home.

One particular evening, she waited for my father to come home. While waiting, she packed our clothes in paper sacks and placed them in a safe spot outside. When my father went home that night, he began to argue with my mother. She had learned a long time ago that she was better off keeping her mouth shut and not say a word. He began to beat her, but she did not hit back. She knew he would stop soon because he was very drunk. My mother said we all watched my father beat her. She told me I was too young to understand, but my sister and brothers cried when our daddy would beat her. My mother knew she had to stop my father one way or another.

After he stopped beating her, he continued to argue and yell. He did not pay any attention to the pot on the stove. She moved backward, looking at my father then at the stove and back to my father to make sure he did not suspect anything. When he sat down at the kitchen table and demanded his dinner, she sweetly told him she made something especially for him. My mother poured the boiling lye on his body and then grabbed me since I was the baby. She ran out of the house with my sister and brothers. She could hear my father shouting at her, threatening to kill her for what she had done, but she kept running with her kids. My father lived, but suffered burns on over thirty percent of his body. He never pressed charges, and he never hit her again. She was forced to leave town because she was afraid of his threats. My mother did not have any family in the city except distant cousins. Both of her parents were dead, only her stepfather was alive.

I made the same recipe, but it was not hot. It sat there as a re-minder to him of what could happen to him. Lucious never said a word to me about the three incidents, and I never mentioned them either. I had to take a stand and make plans to leave without him not knowing, if that was even possible. He stayed so close to home when he did not have any money. I was not myself, but I had enough sense to avoid him by not trying to avenge my pain. I stayed out of his way while attending to the boys' needs, going to work, and paying the bills. Lord, please forgive me. " *Dearly beloved, avenge not your-selves, but rather give place unto wrath: for it is written, Vengeance is mine; I will repay, saith the Lord"* (**Romans 12:19, KJV).**

I continued to try and live my life to the fullest, in spite of my failing marriage. I decided to enjoy the boys as often as possible. It was Jr.'s last year in high school, and we were both excited for him to get out on his own. My mother-in-law called late one night to tell us her father had died; I offered my condolences. Lucious was not in at that time, but I told her I would tell him as soon as he came home. I saw Lucious the next day and told him about his grandfather, but he showed no remorse or concern. I called my mother-in-law back to let her know I had told Lucious the sad news, and we could not afford to attend the out-of-town funeral. She understood. I sent flowers and a card from the family. She called a couple of days later to tell me how much she appreciated the flowers; she knew they had come from me. She had not expected to hear from Lucious, and she was right. I felt terrible to hear to her say that about her son, but it was the truth. When she needed her only son the most, he was not there for her.

In fact, Lucious had always been on the receiving end of the stick in the family being the only male and the youngest. I called my mother to let her know about my mother-in-law's father's death. She said she would call to express her sympathy. My mother-in-law called back and said she needed to talk about the funeral. She said it was brief and was relieved that it was over. He had been on a kidney machine and suffered for months. She ended the call by saying, "He's resting now." She also told me she heard from Lucious. He asked her how she was doing and apologized for not attending the funeral.

Summer was upon us, and Steven was leaving for his grandparent's house for the entire summer. We were both looking forward to him enjoying their company in Missouri. We both needed the separation to miss each other. Most of all, I was happy Steven was getting away from Lucious because he should not be looked at as a father figure – more of as someone who helped to bring him into the world. Lucious was not even around at the time of Steven's birth! When we started breaking up as husband and wife, I used to say Lucious was not Steven's father, only to irritate him. It worked. It is tough to set goals, values, and ground rules for boys, especially when you have a drug addict as a father who was supposed to be the head of the household.

By my faith, I was determined to instill this passage into my boys' hearts: *"For if a man thinks himself to be something, when he is nothing, he deceived himself. But let every man prove his work, and then shall he have to rejoice in himself alone, and not in another"* (**Galatians 6:3-4, KJV**).

Lucious decided he was not going to worry about getting a job and would rather live his life as a crack addict – free and drugged. My birthday came, and I received four plants along with an ice cream cake. I felt good in spirit and soul because I had reached a point in my life of leaving my worries behind and looking toward the future. It was like *"Casting all your anxiety on Him, because He cares for you. Be of sober spirit, be on the alert. Your adversary, the devil, prowls around like a roaring lion, seeking someone to devour. But resist him, firm in your faith, knowing that the same experiences of suffering are being accomplished by your brethren who are in the world. After you have suffered for a little while, the God of all grace, who called you to His eternal glory in Christ, will Himself perfect, confirm, strengthen and establish you. To Him be dominion forever and ever. Amen"* (**1Peter 5:7-11, NASB**).

I often asked Lucious what he wanted out of life, and he told me he had not thought about it as a thirty-three-year-old man I thought he needed to be thinking about something. Whenever, I left him, I thought he might do better for himself, or he might live as a homeless person. He had never been out in the world alone. He always had someone helping him through his everyday life. As time went on, I started visiting friends and neighbors, all the while gritting my teeth at the thought of hearing something about Lucious and his begging. I was thinking about a neighbor who was going through a marriage break up, and I wanted to show support. However, I quickly learned not to try to tell someone what to do when your house is not in order. I sat and listened to my neighbor, and she began to share different incidents that happened between her and her spouse.

As I listened, I drifted off and thought about my situation with Lucious; it all began to sound familiar. I thought I was dreaming while I was awake; I could have told her what to say next. I just smiled and nodded my head trying to show concern. She asked me what I thought, but I told her it wasn't for me to give my opinion because I would have had to have been there from the start of their relationship to share my opinion about what she was facing. I lost track of time and ended up being there for over two hours, but it was necessary. Just being there for my neighbor seemed to be a help. Just before I left, I told her to trust in God and keep the faith as I had learned to do. Because *"He healeth the broken in heart, and bindeth up their wounds"* (**Psalm 147:3, KJV**).

At times, it might seem like everything's going wrong, but you have to remember God doesn't put anything on you that you can't handle. I thank Him every day for each day that harm doesn't come to my boys and me. The Word of God was true for us *" No weapon that is formed against thee shall prosper; and every tongue that shall rise against thee in judgment thou shalt condemn. This is the heritage of the servants of the LORD, and their righteousness is of me, saith the LORD"* (**Isaiah 54:17, KJV**).

It was Memorial Day, and we had friends over – my friends – for a cookout. It was a hot day, but I managed to have a lovely time with my family and friends. Lucious was in the house too, but it was not the same as it used to be. We used to have cookouts all the time, and always had fun together. My friends at the picnic were all of the women I met after Lucious walked out on the boys and me. The atmosphere was different, but fun. Lucious stayed in the other room watching TV. We sat around and shared my marriage stories. They had become a joking matter to keep from crying, I guess, from the school of hard knocks. I told my guests that my biggest fear was going out in public with Lucious and not knowing who we might run into and what they would say to us. To spend time with Lucious and to become a part of his drug life was not a chance I wanted to take. His presence toward me outside the house was life-threatening, and I was only trying to be cautious. I told my friends our problems had been going on for about three years. The time was near when either the marriage would end, or he would get some professional help. I proceeded to tell them I had learned to take my living arrangement one day at a time, forgetting for now that my marriage was over.

While I was sharing my marriage stories, I could tell from the looks on their faces they did not know what to say. They showed empathy, and I was glad they had listened. However, I surprised myself by showing strength while talking about the turmoil I had been through with Lucious; still, I was able to go on.

By sharing my story, I learned they were going through similar situations. One of my friends had a brother who was on crack. She indicated her sister-in-law was going through similar situations with her brother, and she did not know why she was tolerating him. I told her, "You say that now, but you'd say something different after you've experienced it firsthand." We were all married, and I asked each of them a couple of questions: Did we marry for love, support, or both? One said she married for support, and the other said she married for both reasons. Then I asked them if a minister counseled them before marriage, and we all answered, "no." We all agreed we did not know what we were getting into when we said, "I do" to support our spouses or to life's ups and downs. We all laughed and ended our conversation with a smile as they left.

As the summer was upon us, I planned time for myself again. Steven was going to my mother-in-law's and Jr. was old enough to take care of himself. Lucious decided to take Steven to his Mom's house. After all, he was hanging around the house, and we needed a break from him. Steven was excited about the summer trip to his grandparents' house, and they were too. Lucious and Steven were going to travel by train, so I took them to the train station. I was a bit nervous and prayed they made it to their destination safely. My fear was not of the train having an accident as much as Lucious stopping somewhere for drugs with Steven in his care. I walked with them into the train station as they located their seats on the train and watched the train as it left the station and my sight. As soon as I got back home, I telephoned my mother-in-law and asked her to please call me when they arrived. I was worried until she called me the next morning.

She told me my father-in-law was happy to see his son again despite his condition and raggedy appearance. I felt so relieved and was then able to start enjoying my summer as a single mother. I had asked Steven to call me when he arrived at his grandparents' house; he left a message for me on the answering machine the next day.

The weeks passed quickly, and the day came when Lucious was to come back from dropping Steven off at his parent's home in the Midwest. He called around 1:00 a.m. and said that the train had just come into Dallas. He needed me to pick him up. I had purchased the tickets myself, so I knew he was not telling the truth about the train just coming into Dallas that late at night. The train was supposed to arrive by rush hour that day – not after midnight. I knew this, but I thought the train might have been late since I did not receive a telephone call from him. Therefore, I went to the station and found the station closed. I yelled to the security guard on duty and asked him what time the train from St. Louis had arrived. He said the train from St. Louis came in on time at 4:00 p.m. I drove back home, and it was about an hour later when Lucious called again. He said he was still waiting for me to pick him up from the train station. I told him he was not telling the truth because I had just left the closed train station and spoke with the security guard on duty.

Then he said he was at the bus station on Main Street. I told him since he changed his location, he would have to find a way home or walk home. Instead, I decided to go to the bus station against my better judgement. When I got to the bus station, he was there waiting with his luggage on his arm. Lucious had been in Dallas since the arrived train that afternoon and was not telling the truth just as I expected. He had to visit the crack house before coming home; his parents must have given him some money. As we drove back to the house, I told him the only reason I picked him up was because he had taken Steven to his mother's home for me.

Each time I saw a different side of this crack user, I understood he would not change as long as he did not have the willpower to overcome his addiction. Lucious had become a weak case as a crack user and did not plan to change anytime soon since he had fallen in love with the use of crack, falling in love with the joy it brought him. It was apparent Lucious did not have the willpower to overcome this addiction and professional help was needed. But with Jesus we can do all things to survive in this troubled world. *" I have said these things to you, that in me you may have peace. In the world you will have tribulation. But take heart; I have overcome the world"* (**John 16:33, ESV).**

After Steven left, I did not have to cook just keep the house clean. When Lucious asked if I was going to prepare food for him, I told him I was on a summer vacation. Furthermore, I gave up cooking for him a long time ago – he needed to put that message in his crack memory bank. Lucious tended to fantasize about our marriage, thinking everything was all right. The crack cocaine drugs caused him to feel that way.

Jr. and I spent some quality time together that summer while Steven was with his grandparents. Lucious was still taking his trips on Wednesdays and Thursdays to the neighborhood convenience store. I rarely saw him, which was great for me. I often wondered why drug addicts did not hold onto a job to support their habit, instead of begging, borrowing, or stealing. Lucious had stooped so low to get back to earth from the crack adventures that he sometimes ended up in jail for taking things which did not belong to him. The arguments between Lucious and me decreased, in part because Steven was not home.

On the Fourth of July, I decided to cook out after exercising at the health spa. I left Lucious watching the food on the grill. When I returned, the food was burnt. I did not get mad; I just shook it off and cooked something for Jr. and me to eat. It's important to know that when you argue or get upset with a crack addict, you are wasting your time. I tried very hard not to argue with him. I began to notice Lucious' reactions to this. But he had lost his attention span and moved much slower than before crack had become a part of his life. His health was deteriorating at a rapid pace; I was saddened by this because he kept denying he needed professional help. I contacted his doctor at the local VA hospital, and he informed me Lucious aged ten years in his physical health by abusing his body with harsh street drugs. *"Do you not know that your bodies are temples of the Holy Spirit, who is in you, whom you have received from God? You are not your own"* (**1 Corinthians 6:19, NIV**).

Since I had some time on my hands, I decided to enroll in college to take a Spanish course. This course would last for six weeks and was something I had always wanted to pursue. Every time I reported to class, I felt good, like it was where I needed to be. The class benefitted me at work in an area where I had some difficulty. It had been over eight years since my college days of pursuing a bachelor's degree.

I planned my first vacation to go up north alone to visit ex-co-workers and was looking forward to the trip. Jr. was going to drive my car while I was gone. A neighborhood friend dropped me off at the airport since Jr. did not know the way. She honked the horn when she came to the house to take me to the airport. I was leaving, I saw Lucious in the front yard. I had my suitcase, and I will never forget the look on his face when he saw me leaving. I got in the car and my girlfriend said, "Girl, you are bold! Did you see the look on his face? It was like you haven't told him that you were leaving!"

"I didn't tell him anything – and I don't care about the look on his face!" We burst out laughing and joked about Lucious all the way to the airport.

When I got to my vacation spot, the air smelled so fresh. It was as if God had just finished cleaning that part of the earth here up north. For a week, I saw the most beautiful lakes I had ever seen, I rested, went sightseeing, and had a wonderful and well-deserved vacation. It eventually ended, and a part of me wanted to stay while the other part needed to get back to Dallas. Jr. and my neighbor picked me up from the airport. I asked Jr. to brief me on what happened at home during the week that I was away. He said he just rested. The house was the same as I had left it, but we did need bread, milk, and cereal. I felt right at home as the gopher of the family, but I loved it.

Lucious was awake when I arrived home, but he did not say anything to me nor I to him. A couple of days passed before he told me how he felt about me leaving for a week without knowing where I was. I said to him that when he decided to come back home, I had made it very clear that I didn't love him, nor did I care where he went or how he spent his time. All we had was a living arrangement and nothing more. I told him I was going to do what made me happy and enjoy my life without him in it. If he could not accept that, we needed to go our separate ways. Lucious told me he still loved me and had feelings for me.

I told him, "I don't need a confession right now because you don't mean what you say. There is nothing you can say or do now because it does not mean anything to me. I know you are trying to keep up with me, but it will not work. Not now or ever for that matter. Not after all you have continued to do toward our family. Specifically, since you haven't gotten professional help." He said nothing after I finished talking, and just walked away with his head down.

My mother called and wanted to know what was going on. Lucious had called her and said I left him for a week; he did not know where I was. I told her not to worry, because I had gone on a vacation to visit some friends. "Whatever Lucious told you is something he assumes.

I'm going to continue to do the things that make me happy." I assured her everything was alright and began to tell her about my vacation.

It was so hard returning to work after vacation for a week. My first day back seemed so long. After work, I went to the health spa. When I got home from working out, I noticed Steven's TV from the living room was missing. Lucious was nowhere to be found. I waited for Lucious to get home it was late that night when he finally walked in the door. I went to the bedroom where he was sleeping and asked him for the pawn ticket. He said he would keep it and get the TV out the next day. Once again, I repeated myself and asked for the pawn ticket. Once again, he refused to give it to me. I slapped him across the head. He looked at me in disbelief, but he gave me the pawn ticket. I was so angry I wanted to walk away from that house and never look back, but I knew there was always a light at the end of the tunnel.

I did leave the house for a little while, driving around and composing myself by repeating the Lord's Prayer. *"A Prayer of the afflicted, when he is overwhelmed, and pours out his complaint before the LORD. Hear my prayer, O LORD, and let my cry come to You"* (**Psalm 102:1, NKJV).**

Looking back over what the boys and I went through with Lucious' drug addiction, it was a good thing I had joined a church. After starting a weekly Bible study; I not only enjoyed it, but it gave me hope during a time when I had little hope in sight because of the constant battle of dealing with a crack user.

Lucious called me at work the next day to tell me he had some money to get Steven's TV out of the pawnshop. I told him that I had the ticket, so he would have to give me the money. The harsh feelings toward Lucious were still there, and I realized the only way those feelings would leave would be when we were living apart. We had been very lucky up to that point because we had not hurt each other physically, but the mental stress was taking its toll on me. I used to think I could try to forget all that happened and try to mend my broken heart, but it just was not possible since so much had come between us. He wasn't trying to change his ways and continued lying about everything to anyone who would listen. There would be a better, brighter day once I was away from Lucious and able to look back on the marriage that had been unbearable for the past five years.

I got the money from Lucious that evening when I came home from work. Later, I was asleep when Lucious came knocking on my bedroom door.

"Are you going to tell Jr. that the girl in his room needs to leave?" he asked.

"First of all, I wasn't aware that Jr. had a girl in his room. If there's a problem with my son, I'll deal with it," I replied.

He went on to say, "Since you laid up with someone on your weeks' vacation, he feels like he can do it, too." I just smiled and went to Jr.'s bedroom, with Lucious following me. I knocked on his bedroom door, and he immediately opened it. I asked him what was going on, and he explained he was showing his music collection to his girlfriend and listening to a cassette on her headsets. I looked into the room and saw the albums and cassette tapes on the floor, and his girlfriend with her headset on looking scared.

I turned to Lucious and asked him, "What's wrong with this picture?" He ignored me and asked Jr. when the girl was going to leave. Jr. said she had planned to stay until midnight since it was the weekend. Lucious just looked at me and said, "The boy is just bringing girls here and doing whatever he feels like, No respect."

I asked Lucious, "Have you ever seen or heard Jr. do anything in this house that was disrespectful?"

"No," he answered. I told him there was always pleasure-having fun with friends other than him, and especially in a different state. Then I said, "Goodnight and sweet dreams." When I got back to my bedroom, I sat and thought for a moment about Lucious having the nerve to pass judgment not being the man of this house and given his experiences! Nevertheless, this was another chance for him to argue, now it was against Jr. The next morning, Jr. and I had breakfast together; we talked about the previous night's incident. I told him I trusted him, and he knew my feelings about having girls in his bedroom with the door closed. He again assured me it was purely innocent. Most of the time they were girlfriends from school, nothing serious. I left that conversation for the time being, but decided to pay closer attention to both him and Lucious.

Since Steven is on vacation I really miss having him around. When I left the house every day, I felt like I had forgotten something. I came home from work and noticed Lucious was not back. It seemed like he had not been at the house all day. The mail was still in the mailbox. Then I heard a knock at my bedroom door – it was Lucious. I had spoken too soon. He wanted to borrow a safety pin, but I told him he needed to wait until I had my nap. Better yet, go away. It seemed that since I had my vacation, he was always at my door. After my rest, I went to the health spa. Every time I worked out, I was better able to think things out. I decided to contact his probation officer and see what he could do to help Lucious. When I got home from the health spa, Lucious was back.

I asked Lucious, "What do you want to do with the rest of your life?"

"I haven't given that any thought," he answered again.

"Well, when do you plan on giving up drugs and stop living on the edge every day? Do you think I'm going to stay here with you and continue to live like strangers for much longer, especially with you in your present condition?"

"I don't know," he said as he walked away. "Oh yeah, I called a drug treatment center, and they told me to come on Tuesday. I'd like you to go with me."

I told him I needed to think about that. A couple of days passed, and I still did not have an answer for Lucious. Lucious did not forget about my vacation. Although it was over a month ago, it was like my needs were not a priority to him. He started complaining in front of his family about my lack of support for him.

I told him, "Don't try to paint me as the bad gal here, while you're trying to be the saint. It was just a matter of time before your family knew I did not want you and that I was planning to leave you. Who cares about how it looks for your family to know that you are not in my life anymore? However, if you do not like what I have resorted to, then file for a divorce as soon as you get some money. I have no plans to give up any happiness because of what you or your family thinks." He said he needed to think about the divorce, and I asked him to let me know as soon as possible what he was going to do. I proceeded to prepare our dinner, and we did not say anything to each other the rest of the night. *"Anyone who does not provide for their relatives, and especially for their household, has denied the faith and is worse than an unbeliever is"* (**1Timothy 5:8, NIV).**

Lucious did not speak to me for a couple of days. He finally spoke and said he decided to get some professional help, but wanted his parents to go with him instead of me. I said told him that would be best. I felt no remorse or empathy for him at that time. Then I went out to the front yard and began to edge the grass while listening to my gospel music. About twenty minutes later, Lucious came outside to start watering the grass. I asked him to please wait until I was finished edging the grass. I stopped what I was doing, gathered up all the lawn tools, and went into the house to do something else. About thirty minutes later, there was a knock at my bedroom door. It was Lucious telling me I could edge because he was finished watering the grass. I did not respond to his remark because I knew he was in an argumentative mood I did not want to stoop to his level although it was hard for me to keep my peace. *"I find then a law, that, when I would do good, evil is present with me"* (**Romans 7:21, KJV).**

At this point, I had developed a great sense of patience for Lucious and his crack habit. I did some research about crack cocaine and the affect it has on addicts. The mood he was in was a result of me not wanting to be involved with his decision to get professional help.

My in-laws would be in town soon, so I needed to do some general house cleaning again and discuss Lucious' condition with them. A couple of days later, Lucious reminded me he wanted his parents to go to the rehabilitation center with him instead of me. I told him

I understood and I knew this was yet another attempt to win over his parents on another crack manipulation scheme. Lucious' entire attitude changed toward me the closer the day came for his parents to visit. He acted as if he did not need anything from me and had a snobby attitude. I ignored him and whatever he had to say, but I would not back down from defending myself. *"Beware of false prophets, which come to you in sheep's clothing, but inwardly they are ravening wolves"* (**Matthew 7:15, KJV**).

As Jr. and I completed tasks around the house in preparation for my in-laws. Lucious just sat around and watched TV in his bedroom. I did not mind because I needed the time away from him even if he was in the house. I did look for that devil to come out and water the grass again while I was cutting it, but he did not. I came to terms with doing the things that needed to be done, and I began to enjoy it. At this point, I had played the role of the father and mother for years.

One of my sisters-in-law called, and I asked when she expected her parents to get to Dallas. She said she did not know, but if they came to my house first, to tell them to call her. She asked to speak to Lucious, so I handed him the telephone and walked away. During this trip, my in-laws were expecting to help Lucious. I prayed their visit would not be a wasted one or in vain.

My in-laws stayed with us because their daughter's place was too small. I knew it would be a week to remember. They were always welcomed, but I could have done without the bickering. When my in-laws and Steven arrived in Dallas, I was so glad to see him. I left work early only to come home and to find my sister-in-law and her daughter at my home, along with Steven. My mother-in-law prepared dinner, and everyone enjoyed it. Jr. was still at school, but I made a plate for him. Whenever my mother-in-law visited the house belonged to her – I insisted. We had such fun family conversations as we ate and sat around the kitchen table. My in-laws were always buying things for the kids, whether it was their kids or grandkids. Sometimes I got so angry when they bought stuff for their grown kids who never returned the favor by taking them out for dinner or a movie to show their appreciation. The in-laws paid for everything. Since being married to Lucious, he had never offered to pay or treat them to anything. They were always helping us out. Even when we got married, they bought us our first car and some used apartment furniture.

I started staying out of his family conversations. I only listened, because blood is thicker than water. Treating my mother-in-law to lunch or dinner when she came to Dallas showed my appreciation for her generosity. The last time Lucious was at home, his mother brought him a winter coat. She asked him about it. Lucious said he sold it as soon as he got off the train from taking Steven to visit during the summer. He went on to say he sold all the clothing they had bought him. I felt so sorry and had to leave the room; it was the look on my –in-laws' face, especially my mother-in-law. While in my bedroom, I could hear them talk I was glad in a way they had that opportunity; now they could see their son's physical condition.

About an hour later, I returned to the living room and offered my bed to the in-laws. They refused and said they would sleep on the sofa bed. I understood, but I was concerned about their jewelry and money. She told Lucious he had better not take her jewelry, and he assured her he would not. Since my in-laws had been in town, Lucious had not received anything from them. His entire outlook seemed different to me, and we barely said five words to each other. I knew it was for the best because he tended to talk down to me when they were around. The following day, my mother-in-law and sister-in-law were talking at the dining room table. Then my sister-in-law looked at Lucious and said, "Lucious are you craving for crack? Your facial appearance looks different, are you ok?."

I did not say a word because I knew what was going on. It had been three days since my in-laws arrived, and Lucious had been there the entire time. When something was mentioned about Lucious' drug habit, the look on my mother-in-law face was empathy for someone who was hurting. It is hard to imagine the hurt and pain they faced with their only son as a drug addict; addiction is a phenomenon. Every time my in-laws visited, they devoted more of their time and money to nurturing and helping wherever needed; they were god-send parents to the boys and me. *"It is of the LORD'S mercies that we are not consumed because his compassions fail not. They are new every morning: great is thy faithfulness"* (**Lamentations 3:22-23, KJV).**

My in-laws bought Steven another TV and video game, so now we had an extra TV, which was not good at that time. I asked my mother-in-law privately if she wanted to take the extra TV back with her, but she did not. I asked Lucious if he wanted to buy it, but he said he was not going to buy anything from me. I asked my sister-in-law if she wanted to buy it for ten dollars, and she agreed. My mother-in-law asked Lucious why he talked so rudely to me he had nothing to say. I told her since he began his drug addiction, he always spoke rudely to me, especially in front of her. The night before my in-laws were leaving to go back home, we spent some quality time together. She expressed her gratitude to me for putting up with her son, know-ing it had been painful. She stated she realize it was not a good idea to give him any more money or he can't be trusted with anything he can sell.

I did not ask her what had happened to their plan to go to the re-habilitation center . Wasn't that the reason they came to Dallas in the first place? Lucious went into the living room and asked his mother for money to buy a bus ticket. She said she would not give him mon-ey, but she would give some to his sister to buy his ticket. Again, she was on the defensive side, which was a sign of improvement on my in-law's behalf. She stated, "I've never seen a drug addict craving for crack before, and it's a sad sight to see my child this way. He looked like a lizard, with your glassy eyes, and with the way, he moves his tongue. When he started craving for crack, he became very hostile toward his sister. He told her to stay at home for a change because she'd been at our house for a week." I just sat and listened because I knew she needed to talk to someone. I had been there and done that already. As always, I enjoyed my in-laws, but sometimes wished they would stop handing out money every time Lucious needed some. They needed to allow him to get it for himself. Also, they needed to enjoy their vacation for a change when visiting us in this condition.

I did mention to my mother-in-law about my plans to leave Lucious and move on because it had come to that. He wasn't going to help in any way toward the boys and me.

She said, "I can't figure out why you're still living with Lucious."

I told her, "I refuse to allow Lucious and his drug addiction to dictate my move. He will have to leave first. I cannot raise an adult male and respect him as my husband."

Again, she said she did not know why I stayed with him.

"Look," I replied, "I didn't go out and beg Lucious to come back. He came back here, and I will leave at my choosing."

My mother-in-law's response to me was, "But a man and a woman must work together to keep a unified family. If one partner is not helping and is working against the other, the marriage as a whole is a failure. The partner who's working to keep the family together eventually leaves."

I told her, "I agree with what you've said. Thank you." When my mother-in-law bought Steven things like school clothes or video games, I felt they were trying to keep the family together for Lucious' sake. I often told them they did not need to do those things because they felt obligated to do them but to do them as grandparents. They were exceptional people to me, and had always been there for me regardless of their son's failures as a father.

The following day, my in-laws left to go back home, and Lucious left Steven in the house by himself. I had called from work and found out Steven was home alone. I worried, but continued to check on Steven every hour. I told him if he needed anything I was just two minutes away from him. Jr. came by the office and told me Steven was at the house by himself, and he had to go to football practice. He told me, "I have decided to take Steven with me."

"Thank you, Jr. I love you for that, but I'll be home shortly to take care of Steven." I tried not to push Steven off on Jr. unless it was necessary.

Lucious was supposed to go for his outpatient treatment, but he did not. Not expecting too much from him, I told him I would stick around the house until he got professional help. I did what I said. However, since he was taking me for granted, I had no choice but to move on. My mother-in-law called to see if Lucious went to rehab; I told her he did not go. I knew she was disappointed again. However, I knew after she saw Lucious for herself and the condition he was in, she had to turn it over to the Lord and continue to pray for him. When he got home, I told him his mother had called to see if he had gone to the rehabilitation center. In his adult life she was still trying to *"Train up a child in the way he should go: and when he is old, he will not depart from it" (**Proverbs 22:6, KJV**).*

Steven and I were so excited because this was the first day of school. I took off from work to devote my time to the boys' first day of school. I took Steven to school and helped him get settled into class and meet his teacher. Whenever I took an interest in my boys' activities, they seemed to feel good about themselves. I believe it is necessary to be a part of your children's lives, and I was trying to fill the absence in their lives without a father figure. When I completed my morning errands, I returned home, Lucious and his car were not around. His car documents had expired, and it needed some work done on it. He had taken the car without the proper car documents and was driving around only God knows where. If Lucious was caught, he would be put in jail without a doubt. My sister-in-law called, and I told her Lucious had left in the car. She told me she was going to come and take the car because he did not need to be driving it. She went on to say she was so tired of him hurting their Mom and Dad. Then I told her he did not go to the rehabilitation center either. She said she was tired of Lucious lying and not caring about anybody but himself, and then she hung up. I tried to speak as little as possible because she tended to misinterpret me.

I noticed Steven had stopped asking Lucious for anything. In the past, I overheard him asking him to play ball when Lucious was watching a track and field show on TV. Lucious would say the show was more important. I stopped telling Steven to play with his father or go to him for anything. When I heard that, I did not say anything to him about his remark, but I could not see him denying Steven any of his time since he did not work or do anything to make him tired. My oldest son stopped going to Lucious a long time ago because he said he did not like him and did not have anything to say to him. He only listened to Lucious and his drug action stories. Jr. was protecting Steven and myself from Lucious in his own way by listening to his drug stories.

Lucious continued to drive his car without the proper documents, and my mother-in-law continued to call to check up on him. Even hundreds of miles away from him, she still worried about him and when he was going to change. He had not come home for a couple of days; it was always a pleasure when he was not around. Every time he got some money, it was like a holiday for the boys and me because Lucious was not around. I knew there would be a brighter day soon. When he came home, he would wash up and sleep off whatever he smoked the day before. After he awoke from sleeping off his crack high, he told me he went to rehab. They wanted him to stay for twenty-eight days on a work program. He needed to do that. I told him that was good for him if he followed through with it. However, I would have to see it to believe it.

I got a part-time job, and Steven was welcome to come with me when I worked. When I got home one day, Jr. told me Lucious had called collect and needed to have his car towed.

"Thank you, Jr.. Remember, we don't accept collect calls from Lucious or anyone else."

"I know, Mom, but it happened so fast. Before I knew it, I was talking to him. He gave me the number of where he was."

"Well," I said, "throw the telephone number away because I do not plan on calling him especially in that part of town."

Lucious called again later that night, but his call was not a collect call. He asked me to come and pick him up, and have his broken car towed with the towing vehicle service I had purchased.

I told him, "Please do not bother me again with your problems, and I will not get involved with you ever again outside of this house." Lucious tended to take me for granted, he would overlooked what . . . I said to him. For the last six months or more, Lucious had only been an adult burden on me and needed to be responsible for his adult actions. I did not help Lucious that night.

It was time to cut the grass again, so Jr. and I decided to take care of it. While we were in the yard, Lucious came out and told Jr. he had called collect because he was trying to con the operator into giving him another free call. He said he had the operator send him some money to the house because he lied to get it. Lucious told the operator that he was calling long distance and lost his money in the telephone machine, so the operator told him she would have to send it to his home.

Jr. said he was going to try that too, but I told him, "Don't listen to someone who steals and takes everyone and everything for granted – someone who's a crack addict. " *It is out of the heart that evil thoughts come, as well as murder, adultery, sexual immorality, stealing, false testimony, and slander*" (**Matthew 15:19, ISV).**

I continued, "Don't look up to people who only tell you how to be dishonest. You will only end up in jail and ruin your life. If you don't believe me, look at Lucious." More and more, I was convinced I had to leave Lucious because his ways were a terrible influence on the boys. When a child is exposed to drugs and stealing in his home, he will learn from that, try it himself, and end up in jail for the rest of his life.

The next day, Steven and I went to Sunday school. My bedroom door was left unlocked. When I got home, I noticed it was open and inventoried everything. All was there, including Lucious. I did not know Lucious went into my bedroom and searched through my things until two days later when Steven wanted to join the cub scouts at school. I told him to ask his father to pay half the amount of his admission fee. When he asked him, Lucious told Steven to go back and say he did not have any money. He also told Steven he was tired of me sending him into the living room to ask for money. Then I walked into the living room, and we started shouting at each other because I did not appreciate what he said to Steven.

"How can you be a father if you always turn Steven down, no matter what he asks? You pawn his toys, you didn't tell him the truth about taking him to the movies and you sit around all day and do nothing. When he asks for help, you turn him down, and you are a worthless man."

Lucious said, "I don't like how you're putting my business on the street, treating me like I don't exist."

"As far as I'm concerned, you don't exist," I replied. "And as far as putting your so-called business in the street, you should have thought about that before you embarrassed your family in front of the entire neighborhood for the last two years."

"Well, I don't like the fact you are locking your bedroom door and all of your things inside it," he said.

"You should know by now that I don't care how you feel. Your opinion means nothing to me as long as you're living here with the boys and me."

Then he said, "You told me you would wait until I recovered from rehab . . ."

"I have waited, Lucious, and you haven't shown any improvement since you've been out of prison. What have you done to better your condition since you got out of jail?"

"Nothing," he admitted.

"What have you done to support your family?" He did not respond right away to that question either.

Then he said, "I'm supporting you and the boys by paying half of the house payment."

"If you were supporting the boys and me as a husband and father, you would be paying the entire house payment. Where would you be if you did not pay to stay somewhere? Now, we need to sell this house and get on with our lives living separately. I'll call another realtor, and maybe this time we can get someone to finance." I had been planning that conversation for a long time, so I was prepared for the discussion to end with a bitter ending.

Thanksgiving was upon us, and I had planned to cook enough food for the company we were expecting. The boys were out of school, and

I was off from work for a couple of days. We had so many reasons to be thankful. Lucious was still out smoking crack and not having much to do with the boys or me. However; I knew it was just a matter of time before we left Lucious and began a new life. Jr. and Steven told me what they wanted for Christmas, and I was prepared to purchase them.

I asked Lucious, "Are you going to help me with buying Steven's Christmas gifts?"

He told me, "Mind your own business."

"Well, will you at least give me some extra money for the Thanksgiving dinner since you do keep your money?"

"You're doing just fine," he said. "So, don't ask me for anything else."

"Thank you, Lucious. Have a nice Thanksgiving holiday." I managed to buy everything I had planned, and we had a lovely time. We ate until we could not eat anymore. My mother called and wished the family and me a Happy Thanksgiving and told me to keep the faith, I said Okay.

I invited Lucious to join us at the dinner table. He could not say anything, but he knew something was up because of the expression on my face.

I told him, "It has been a pleasure living with you. We have a lot to be thankful. Now, I have a surprise for you, but you are going to have to wait until after dessert. And I want to take a picture of you when I give you your surprise."

As soon as he finished eating, I smiled (Kodak moment) and gave him a letter. Lucious was lost for words. I had given him a copy of a letter that indicated I had power of attorney over him and I was going to have him committed. He jumped up from the table and ran out of the house – I never saw him move so fast. In fact, we did not hear from Lucious for a couple of days until he called collect to tell us he was in jail. Lucious had been picked up for soliciting outside of the jail parking lot downtown; he was telling everyone he was the parking attendant and persuaded the people who were visiting someone in jail to pay him for parking. Lucious was sentenced to six months.

I said, "okay, I'll call your parents." Then I hung up.

I immediately called Lucious' lawyer and told her about him being back in jail. I also told her about the phony power of attorney letter.

She told me, "Be careful. Now, what do you want me to do about Lucious?"

"Look," I said, "Lucious has been in and out of jail for years. Once he gets out of jail, he has to go back to that drug-infested area to meet his probation officer. If you want to help, please talk to my in-laws so you can get a clear picture of Lucious' background. After that, if time permits, please call me back. If you cannot then know this: I need my husband to get some long-term professional help. Please see what you can do to have him sent to a rehabilitation center that will help him and not just keeps him off the streets so that he can dry out."

Three days later, Ms. Daily, the court-appointed lawyer, called and said, "Lucious has been sentenced to a six months rehabilitation center. This center has an 80% success rate of recovering drug addicts. However, Lucious cannot have any family visits for the first two months. Afterwards, you and the boys will need to go through a group counseling session. The rehab center will contact you seven weeks from today."

I contacted the family on both sides to keep them aware of Lucious' progress whenever I heard anything. Boy, time just flew by, and the day I had dreaded finally came: Lucious was due to have visitors. I resented going because I wanted Lucious to stay longer, and to tell the truth, I had gotten used to living without him.

Steven and I had to attend a group counseling session every Saturday for four weeks at the rehabilitation center; this was designed to prepare us for a changed family member. Each session lasted for a couple of hours, and we had time to observe the other people who attended. After the counseling session, Steven got a chance to visit with his father. Jr. did not participate in any of the meetings.

I was still upset and angry about having to go through the process for Lucious. It seemed like we had been giving up our time to accommodate him once again. Saturday was the only day we could visit, thank God. After that, Lucious was able to come home on weekend passes. So there I was again – off to accommodate him! I hated to be around him. Our conversations were short, and Lucious mainly talked to Steven. I just listened. I felt like I had to babysit my husband, a grown man.

When he got home, he had to check in with his counselor. He was allowed to visit us for 48 hours at a time, and we were all able to attend church together. Before Sunday, though, we had to buy him decent clothing because the clothes he had came from either the Salvation Army rehab center.

When my in-laws came to Dallas for a visit, Lucious got another weekend pass. We all went to church together. I remember the expression on Lucious' face as he listened to the preacher's message that particular Sunday. His face was dark brown and ashy, his eyes were glassy, and he looked as swollen as if a bee had stung him. As he sat and listened to the message, he began to look around the church as if he did not belong there. I wanted to observe Lucious because I had to decide whether to welcome him home or leave him. *"And be not conformed to this world: but be ye transformed by the renewing of your mind, that ye may prove what that good is, and acceptable, and perfect, will of God"* (**Romans 12:2, KJV**).

Lucious was finally able to come home permanently based on his good behavior at the rehabilitation center. He got a job at a radiator shop, making minimum wage. He worked there for about three weeks until the employment office helped him get a better job at a lumber company. We began to work together as a family after taking it one day at a time with our relationship. Lucious joined the church the boys and I were attending. I prayed for peace a long time and wanted to get out of this marriage. However, it never happened so I continue to pray for peace within this home and marriage as I hoped for better days. *"But, my God shall supply all your need according to his riches in glory by Christ Jesus"* (**Philippians 4:19, KJV**).

Lucious continued to work at the lumber company for about three years. Within that time period, we had another child - a girl this time. He also became a deacon at the Baptist church where we all attended. Also, he enrolled in one of the Community Colleges to study to become a drug counselor. The family that prays together stays together. With God's help, life's trials and tribulations help will reaffirm your faith and belief in Him. As the days and years have come and gone while living with Lucious, my mind would ponder over a part of our marriage vows: *for better or for worse.* As we headed to church as a family, I also reflected on my grandmother's and mother's tradition of taking us to the Baptist church.

Oh, what sweet memories!

BAPTIST CHURCH TRADITION

By
Avis Lamb Brown

EARLY RISE SUNDAY MORNINGS.

STUMBLING INTO EACH OTHER, WHILE DRESSING OUR SUNDAY BEST

MOMMA I CAN'T FIND MY…. I NEED THIS …

THE AROMA OF BREAKFAST WE WOULDN'T DARE MISS

AFTER BREAKFAST OFF TO THE BAPTIST CHURCH IN OUR NEIGHBORHOOD

BEING WELL BEHAVED AS WE HAVE BEEN TAUGHT WE SHOULD

CHILDREN ARE SEEN NOT HEARD

SAID BY OUR PARENTS, "I BETTER NOT HEAR A MUMBLING WORD FROM YOU!"

THREE HOURS LATER CHURCH STILL GOING STRONG.

PARENTS SAID NOT A MUMBLING WORD

BUT I WILL, PRAY TO GOD, AND ASK HOW LONG.

"And I also say unto thee, That thou art Peter, and upon this rock, I will build my church; and the gates of hell shall not prevail against it"
(Matthew 16:18, KJV).

Chapter Five

What are your thoughts after reading Chapter Five?

_____
_____
_____
_____
_____
_____
_____
_____
_____
_____

Have you ever experienced this in your family?

_____
_____
_____
_____
_____
_____
_____
_____
_____

Do you know someone who is going through a similar situation?

_____
_____
_____
_____
_____
_____
_____

_____

_____

_____

What can you do to help or how can you be of support to an abuser?

_____

_____

_____

_____

_____

_____

_____

_____

_____

My thoughts about Chapter Five - God is showing the family *"In everything we do, we show that we are true ministers of God. We patiently endure troubles and hardships and calamities of every kind"(**2 Corinthians 6:4-5, NLT**).

Who do we blame, if anyone?

_____

_____

_____

_____

_____

_____

_____

_____

_____

_____

Do you believe in God and has he brought you out of life situations that you needed to escape? Share your testimony.

_____
_____
_____
_____
_____
_____
_____
_____
_____
_____

"Trust in the Lord with all your heart, and do not lean on your own understanding. In all your ways acknowledge him, and he will make straight your paths" (**Proverbs 3:5-6, ESV).**

The Power to Overcome Drug Abuse

AS THE DAYS have come and gone, living with Lucious, my mind continued to ponder over part of our marriage vows for better or for worse. How much better or worse should we as individuals accept from each other? How many times should we forgive each other for the trials and tribulations we've face? After agreeing to give Lucious another chance in our marriage, I have became more aware of what a marriage is all about. We got married at a very young age, right out of college and in love. We did not know where we were going, but we were going together. Now, I was forced to accept I must get to know my husband all over again without recalling the hurt and tremendous pain he caused. Striving to be a better person, I prayed for inner peace and patience to be able to overlook the destruction Lucious caused in our marriage. There were so many things I needed to forgive that it reminded me of the Scripture when *"Peter came to Jesus and asked, 'Lord, how many times shall I forgive my brother or sister who sins against me? Up to seven times?' Jesus answered, 'I tell you, not seven times, but seventy-seven times'* **(Matthew 18:21-22, NIV).**

Sometimes, Lucious and I discussed the issues that involved dealing with the kids and the house. But I quickly found myself stating what was on my mind and standing firm on my decisions. Living the role of a single parent but still married definitely matured me in many ways. However, I had to learn to communicate with Lucious again, accepting his opinions and no longer making decisions on my own. It would take time to heal and trust a recovering adulterer and drug addict.

Lucious was still attending college striving to become a drug counselor. He should do well in this area based on his personal experience. I wrote a book and self-published about our ordeal in dealing with a crack addict and surviving the experience. While marketing my book, I spoke at various rehabilitation centers including the last recovery center where Lucious was a client. After speaking to various groups about Lucious' crack addiction, it reaffirmed drugs are active and real, and have a negative impact on families by destroying the family dynamics.

I had not intended to write this book, but *To God be the Glory*, I did. This book is not my book, but a journey or obligation I felt was given to me by my heavenly Father. I started out writing a journal after facing so much turmoil while dealing with Lucious and his drug addiction. Some of my immediate family were in full support of the book. However, some were not as receptive because drugs were a part of our upbringing in the projects of Miami, Florida. During some of my speaking engagements sharing my experience dealing with an crack addict. I began to feel different with a inner peace and a thankful heart. I found myself speaking with a motherly tone, genuinely concerned about her family who had been affected by drugs, and determined to make an educational impact.

Talking with family members of drug addicts, it disturbs me to see the hurt and pain in their eyes, their body language. I noticed their mannerisms when asking questions about my story. Some even wore sunglasses because they were too ashamed to be seen. I would reply with my motherly tone and with my hand reaching out to them. I tried to reiterate that I was once in their shoes and wore that same face full of pain, disappointment, hurt, and resentment against my loved one. Each volunteer meeting was strengthened because the families needed someone who had walked their same path, yet had a smile on their face through it all. Who would have thought I would be sharing my painful story with strangers? *To God be the Glory.*

Because of all the initial speaking engagements, I was invited to local radio stations in the Dallas area and spoke to different families and friends. The most rewarding meetings happened while talking to the men and women in drug recovery centers and prisons. One day I received a letter from a prisoner being held near Houston, Texas. He invited me to come and speak about the first book I published, My Friend, My Lover, My Husband. He contacted me after reading a copy that was available inside of his prison unit. I responded by reaching out to the chaplain of that prison unit. Days later, I received a call from the chaplain. We communicated for several weeks regarding the protocol about prison life and what I should wear once my background check was cleared.

However, weeks passed after my last conversation with the prison chaplain. Then I received a call and a letter about what I could and could not wear. He went on to tell me that I had been accepted to talk to the prison unit at the request of a prisoner (I had never met) yet received a written invitation to speak about my book. I told the chaplain I had a female friend who would accompany me to talk to the prisoners. She submitted her identification as requested by the chaplain and later that week she was also approved to enter the prison. I told my girlfriend we were cleared to visit the prison unit the following week. I told her I was curious about going because I had never visited Lucious while he was in prison. I went looking for something, but I cannot tell you what.

My appointment was after the prisoners' lunch, and the trip was over three hours. During the three-hour drive to the prison. I told my friend I was looking forward to going and that one of my brothers was in and out of jail for drugs. I never asked my mother or mother-in-law how they felt to have a child locked up for years and only able to communicate with them by letter. My friend shared that she knew some people who were in and out of prison and had visited them while they were in. When we arrived at the prison unit near Houston, Texas, there were several units. We had to stop and ask for the prison unit where I was to speak. Once we got to the parking lot of the prison unit, we saw a tall tower with guards on duty. They instructed us to put our drivers' license in a white bucket pail. After they lifted the bucket back up and checked our identification they returned our licenses in the bucket. They told us to enter through the chain link fence which would lead us to the unit where the chaplain was waiting.

As we entered the fenced area and headed toward the white building (sanctuary), the chaplain who I had communicated with for over a month was there to meet us. He told us to follow him. As we walked behind him, he informed us that four trustee inmates would be escorting us throughout our visit at the prison. The chaplain took us to his office to brief us on the meeting location and how long I was allowed to talk to the group. Then he took us to the sanctuary. As we were walking through the hallway, I looked for a clock for some reason and pictures or something on the walls, but there were no decorations within the facility. While observing the empty partition and preparing my heart to share a word that would bless the inmates, I felt like I was in bondage and needed the Lord's help to say the right things. This situation was just as if Jesus said it would be: *"But when they deliver you up, take no thought how or what ye shall speak: for it shall be given you in that same hour what ye shall speak"* **(Matthew 10:19, KJV**).

When we entered the church sanctuary, it was full of the unit inmates waiting to hear me talk about my book and dealing with a crack addict. The chaplain introduced me to the prisoner who invited me as we entered the sanctuary. We nodded at each other because there was no communication of any kind allowed in the prison especially with a female in the male unit. Then the chaplain introduced me to the rest of the inmates. As I was walked to the podium, I saw a bird sitting in the back of the church that was behind me as I faced the inmates during my talk. I thanked the prisoner who invited me, without saying his name, and the chaplain for the invitation to talk briefly about my experience living with a drug addict and how we overcame.

I was somewhat nervous and curious at the same time because there was such a strange feeling being in that prison environment. As I spoke about my ordeal living with a crack addict the bird that I saw earlier began to fly around behind me. I talked about the feeling that we as family members go through when a loved one brings us so much anger, bitterness, and grief while addicted to drugs and alcohol. I shared with them how my father was a functioning alcoholic for years and how he died from cirrhosis of the liver. At the closing of my presentation, I gave the men encouraging words and told them their actions were because of their drugs of choices but there was still hope in the Lord. *"Fear not, for I am with you; be not dismayed, for I am your God; I will strengthen you, I will help you, I will uphold you with my righteous right hand"* (**Isaiah 41:10, KJV).**

When I was finished with my presentation the chaplain, my friend, and the four trustee inmates walked back to the chaplain's office while the inmates went back to their cells. The chaplain asked me if I had any questions before leaving. I told him I did not. However, out of curiosity, I did not see any clocks on the walls. He said it was not needed when prisoners only got but time. I asked him about dressing from head to toe in my garment. He said it was for my protection; some men had been locked up for a very long time, and they only needed to see my head and hands while talking to them. He went on to say that prison life is a world within itself and specific protocol was followed for the safety of their guest, by assigning four trustees to guard us during our visit.

I said, "WOW!" With that, I was ready to go. We thanked him again for the invitation. He extended a welcome and instructed me to discontinue the communication with the prisoner who invited me to speak. I told him I understood. While putting the situation into the hands of the Lord, I realized *"The LORD will keep you from all evil; he will keep your life. The LORD will keep your going out and your coming in from this time forth and forevermore"* (**Psalm 121:7-8, ESV).**

On our way home from the prison visit my friend and I talked about what we had just experienced between those prison walls, and how thankful we were that our mistakes did not cause us to become a property of the state. I thought about all the years of dealing with Lucious and how bold I was when the drug dealer came to my home. WHAT IF, just what if things had turned out the wrong way and WHAT IF I did something to Lucious to cause me to end up in prison? I asked my friend what the bird was doing while I was speaking. She said it was flying side to side but never landed. I told her at first I was a little nervous, but I kept on talking while it was flying in the back of me. I don't think I will ever forget my experience that day or nor the inmate who invited me. I felt sorry for him because he didn't have long to live based on the crime he had committed while a free man. This incident reminded me of the following Scripture: *"You have heard that it was said, 'AN EYE FOR AN EYE, AND A TOOTH FOR A TOOTH.' But I say to you, do not resist an evil person: but whoever slaps you on the right cheek, turn the other to him also. If anyone wants to sue you and take your shirt, let him have your coat also"* (**Matthew 5:38-40, NASB).**

I continued speaking to whomever would listen to my story dealing with a drug addict and how we overcame it, with the Lord's help. My presentation to them included an apron with three **crooked pockets**, which hold a **small pocket mirror**, **Philips/flat head screwdriver**, and a **measuring tape**.

The **small pocket mirror** symbolized looking at ourselves first as family members realizing our loved one is a drug addict, and that it does not need to be kept in the closet. Remember that when your loved one became addicted to the drug of choice, it did not start in your closet! Develop the following behaviors:

1- Prayer team
2- Show tough love through prayer
3- Stand firm on the Word of God
4- Prayer and communication with the family is critical
5- Pray and do not develop a blame game
6- Sway when the storms come your way
7- Pray for an earthly provision (facility) to get help and watch God change things

It is important to remember we all have a choice in the direction we take as individuals. When Lucious decided to leave his family without warning and no support, I had to accept my responsibilities and rearrange my lifestyle. I had to schedule my plans to continue to live without him. I did not care about going without as long as my kids were taken care of. I refused to allow Lucious to dictate how I lived when *he* was the one on drugs. When you learn to love yourself and no longer have a personal battle within yourself, the enemy outside of you can no longer do harm. Put on the whole armor or God so, you can become stronger and better at loving your drug-addicted family member. *"He that loveth not knoweth not God; for God is love. In this was manifested the love of God toward us, because that God sent his only begotten Son into the world, that we might live through him"* (*1 John 4:8-9, KJV*).

Now, the double-headed, **Philips flathead screwdriver** served its purpose. After Lucious walked out on us and left me alone with two small children in a new city, I developed an attitude as big as Texas. I was so angry with men in general that I wanted nothing to do with them. Stress and resentment set in my heart and my mind. I gained weight, very seldom smiled, and cried all of the time; I had a very long and lonely pity-party. When my health started breaking down – not to mention seeing my children's embarrassment in the neighborhood because of their father's drug addiction – I had to wake up and get myself together.

The **screwdriver** was my symbol for the adjustment we had to make. I became more active in studying the Lord's Word and learning how He wanted us to lean on Him and turn our lives over to him. I noticed a change in my attitude toward Lucious and began to feel good about myself again. When I found myself thinking about the past and the bitterness he caused, I had to adjust my attitude and focus on God. The **screwdriver** could never measure up to God, but I was not at that point in my spiritual life to receive how good God really is and what He can do. I understood the symbol of the **screwdriver** played a major part in my life when I had to fix things around the house and make necessary adjustments for the boys and me. The **screwdriver** had an effect on our family: *"For the word of God is alive and active. Sharper than any double-edged sword, it penetrates even to dividing soul and spirit, joints and marrow; it judges the thoughts and attitudes of the heart"* (**Hebrews 4:12, NIV).**

Finally, the **measuring tape** symbolized how much pain and suffering we, as family members, accept from our drug-addicted loved ones throughout the years.

The Immeasurable

By
Avis Lamb Brown

The immeasurable love we have for our loved ones.

The immeasurable excuses we have heard from our loved ones.

The immeasurable monetary costs we had to pay for a loved one.

**The immeasurable embarrassment the entire family
endured due to a loved one.**

**The immeasurable adjustments the family had to make
without the loved one.**

**The immeasurable friction between the families
because of the loved one.**

The immeasurable loss of some of our loved ones to drugs.

Through this whole drug addiction ordeal there is only One who can measure how much He loved us when He sent His only begotten **SON** so we can have a right to the tree of **LIFE.**

To GOD be the GLORY

God's Love and Ours

"Dear friends, let us love one another, for love comes from God. Everyone who loves has been born of God and knows God. Whoever does not love does not know God, because God is love. "This is how God showed his love among us: He sent his one and only Son into the world that we might live through him. This is love: not that we loved God, but that He loved us and sent his Son as an atoning sacrifice for our sins."

"Dear friends, since God so loved us, we also ought to love one another. No one has ever seen God; but if we love one another, God lives in us and his love is made complete in us.

This is how we know that we live in him and he in us: He has given us of his Spirit. And we have seen and testified that the Father has sent His Son to be the Savior of the world. If anyone acknowledges that Jesus is the Son of God, God lives in them and they in God. And so we know and rely on the love God has for us.

God is love. Whoever lives in love lives in God, and God in them. This is how love is made complete among us so that we will have confidence on the day of judgment: In this world we are like Jesus. There is no fear in love. But perfect love drives out fear, because fear has to do with punishment. The one who fears is not made perfect in love.

*We love because he first loved us. Whoever claims to love God yet hates a brother or sister is a liar. For whoever does not love their brother and sister, whom they have seen, cannot love God, whom they have not seen. And he has given us this command: Anyone who loves God must also love their brother and sister" (**1 John 4: 7-21, NIV).**

Recovery Process

During my presentation to those recovering men and women, I wanted to give them something to think about from a family member's perspective of dealing with an addict. I had many clients at the recovery centers thank me for enlightening them on how drugs affected their families and how much trouble their choices had caused. I continually learned new terms from the ongoing drug rehabilitation due to drugs, such as recovery, codependent, transition, and one day at a time. These words not only relate to a drug user's experience, but also the affected family's experience. *"But, he said to me, 'My grace is sufficient for you, for my power **is** made perfect in weakness.' Therefore I will boast all the more gladly about my weaknesses, so that Christ's power may rest on me"* (**2 Corinthians 12:9, NIV**).

Recovery is defined as "to regain something or restore." Not only do recovering addicts regain themselves in society, but their families also must regain their presence back into the family. *"It may be that the Lord will look upon my misery and restore to me his covenant blessing instead of his curse today"* (**2 Samuel 16:12, NIV**).

Codependent is as "assisting or enabling an addict in their addiction" (the addict's family/friend). Codependent reminds me of how families come together to welcome a new family member to the family with gifts and love. The negative experiences of a recovering addict's loved ones are a slow healing process before some family members are able to open their arms and hearts again. *"I can do all this through him who gives me strength"* (**Philippians 4:13, ESV**).

The transition is defined as "a change from one condition to another." This word convicted me. After I could no longer handle the hurt involved with a drug addict loved one, I decided to turn it over to the Lord. I had transitioned from being the angry wife, mother, and lover toward my husband. My feelings of resentment toward my husband for the years of pain he caused our family changed into patience and resilience toward the entire drug addiction situation. Then I transitioned into accepting the drug problem and reacting positively by finding a positive solution with God's guidance. Not only will the addict become a changed person, but the affected family members will too. The transition is profound, especially when you have to change in certain situations whether you like it or not. *"Do not conform to the pattern of this world, but be transformed by the renewing of your mind. Then you will be able to test and approve what God's will is— His good, pleasing and perfect will"* (**Romans 12:2, NIV**).

One day at a time defines taking each day with caution because dwelling on the past is a trip. Focus on the here and now by taking each day as it comes. If not, you will lose -- family, dignity, self-respect, self-esteem, morals, patience, temptation (especially to drugs), and dependence on God. To put it simply as an innocent child depends exclusively on its parents. At this time, our three-year-old daughter, Jamesa, developed an attitude and tried it on each member of the family. I corrected her in every possible way and whenever she saw me, she was happy and asked for everything. It was as though she was thinking, "I know Momma is going to provide for me." Through it all, she did not have a worry in the world. She took each day at a time to be a child, depending on her family to provide and care for her needs. We should rely and focus on the Lord every second, minute, and hour of the day. *"The Lord is my rock and my fortress, and my deliverer, My God, my rock, in whom I take refuge; My shield and the horn of my salvation, my stronghold"* (**Psalm 18:2, NASB**).

The Cost of a Recovery Process

How much time does your family spend dealing with any type of recovery?

_____
_____
_____
_____
_____
_____
_____
_____
_____
_____

Have you pursued any counseling to help with the recovery process?

_____
_____
_____
_____
_____
_____
_____
_____
_____

"I have told you these things, so that in me you may have peace. In this world you will have trouble. But take heart! I have overcome the world" **(John 16:33, NIV).**

One Day at a Time

By

Avis Lamb Brown

Recovering drug addicts

Without the drugs, what makes you tick?

Taking one day at a time

To allow our minds to grasp society and unwind

Day to day activities, taking all in a stride

Accomplishments, goals, standing focus in recovery will arrive.

Depending on drugs to ease your pain

Over the weeks, months, and years brought to shame.

As humans, we will make mistakes

Once you decide to clean up your act, you find out

There's a whole lot that's at stake.

Fear comes to mind as you unwind,

Being unique, a beautiful person God makes you one-of-a-kind.

Hurt you brought to your families and friends

The 12-step tells you how to mend.

Forgive yourself before you forgive your sister and brother

God holds you accountable – not your father or mother.

One day at a time, one day at a time

Always pray to the One in control of your time and mind.

"Let us then approach God's throne of grace with confidence, so that we may receive mercy and find grace to help us in our time of need" **(Hebrews 4:16, NIV).**

Chapter Six

What are your thoughts after reading Chapter Six?

_____

_____

_____

_____

_____

_____

_____

_____

_____

_____

Have you ever experienced this in your family?

_____

_____

_____

_____

_____

_____

_____

_____

_____

Do you know someone who is going through a similar situation?

_____

_____

_____

_____

_____

_____

_____

_____
_____
_____

What can you do to help or how can you be a supporter of the abusers?

_____
_____
_____
_____
_____
_____
_____
_____
_____

My thoughts about Chapter Six - God is showing the family "*Because of the* Lord'*s great love we are not consumed, for his compassions never fail. They are new every morning; great is your faithfulness. I say to myself, "The* Lord *is my portion; therefore I will wait for him"* **Lamentations (3:22-24, NIV).**

Who do we blame, if anyone?

_____
_____
_____
_____
_____
_____
_____
_____
_____

Do you believe in God and has He brought you out of life situations you needed to escape? Share your testimony.

_____

_____

_____

_____

_____

_____

_____

_____

_____

_____

"Have mercy upon me, O God, according to thy lovingkindness: according unto the multitude of thy tender mercies blot out my transgressions" (**Psalm 51:1, KJV**).

Transition

By
Avis Lamb Brown

Webster's dictionary defines transition

As passage of travel from one point to another.

You, the passenger, unique one-of-a-kind, there is no other,

Your path and destiny detoured

Society's invitation had you lured.

Some say life is not fair, but who has the right to compare

When all people contribute and share.

Your family and friends await with anticipation

The time is now to start over – oh no, it's not too late

Time stands still for no one

Who's to say when your life has begun?

God is our creator who provides whatever we need

Please

When life's uncertainty comes your way,

Stand still, take a deep breath, and ask yourself

"What would Jesus do and say?"

He already did what He wanted to do for us; He gave up His life

I guarantee you, with His Guidance He will see you through

I pray you reach your endeavors and goal . . .

But remember Who's in control.

*"Do not conform to the pattern of this world, but be transformed
by the renewing of your mind. Then you will be able to test and
approve what God's will is—his good, pleasing and perfect will"*
(Romans 12:2, NIV).

A Family's Victorious Defeat Over a Drug Addiction

YEARS OF DEALING with Lucious's drug addiction seeking professional help for him and counseling for the boys and me. I tried to make sense of how and why this drug ordeal happened to my family. Where did we go wrong in our marriage? Could I have done something differently? After identifying with the how's, when's, where's and why's, there will always be some unanswered questions. Crack cocaine is a drug of choice. Many family members found it very cheap to purchase, but paid a higher cost in death and loss of dignity and respect. The benefit of using a substance that damages relationships does not equal the value of the family members who are affected.

During the years of trying to find a solution to the crack addiction problem, we went about it all wrong. There were many mixed feelings and assumption entangled in the crack-addicted issues. My actions were for personal gain disregarding how the other person(crack addict) would feel or do not care. We did not know how to dress for the battle to defend ourselves while dealing with a crack addict or drug user. A person can get caught up in trying to hide the shame and embarrassment brought to your entire family. We were concerned with what people had to say instead of seeking. Who had control over every situation in our lives from the beginning?

My heart has a new ache that feels so good and I must share with you; yes, your heart can ache for good instead of evil. I learned to tap into the *Source* who can handle every problem that arises in my family. Looking back over Lucious's crack ordeal, I asked myself for the first time. 'Why not me?' My family and I have learned to lean not to our own understanding, but unto God. Psalms 23 comes to mind as I often think about what we endured with a drug user and how we came out of the ordeal victoriously. We strayed away from the *Shepherd,* and now we are back to share how we found our way back to the *Shepherd.*

"The LORD is my shepherd; I shall not want" **(Psalm 23:1, KJV)**

Webster's Dictionary defines a shepherd as, "a leader of a flock that tends to the flocks every need on a daily basis." If you stay focused on the *Shepherd,* you will remain on course and not stray away or want for anything. He will take care of your every need again and again. While trying to deal with a crack addict, I strayed away from the *Shepherd* – grandmother's teaching about the Lord - and worked to handle it my way. I grew up knowing about the Lord through my grandmother and mother, but I thought I could deal with the trials and tribulations in my marriage by myself. I dealt with the highs and lows of my feelings and sheltering my kids from any pain and the shame Lucious brought into our home.

I was going through the motion of trying to put out fires in the family that reignited daily. Problems grew more significant over time because I was working to handle something that was too big to do alone. The crack ordeal affected me physically to the point of seeking medical attention. I was advised to get myself together health wise and alleviate whatever was causing the stress in my life. My diagnosis was a tumor on my pituitary gland which is located on the left side outside of the brain. Medication was prescribed to shrink the tumor while managing any stressful situations in my life. To lessen my stress activities, I joined a local family gym to work out the stress and tension that had been building up for years. Eventually, the tumor decreased, and I was taken off the medication.

Lucious and I started attending church on a regular basis, working and taking care of the boys and working out at the local gym. I felt something was still missing but could not quite figure it out. As the boys and I started to get involved in church activities, I began to feel a sense of defeat while dealing with a crack addict. Everything started to take a toll on my body physically not to mention the sanity of the relationship between the boys and Lucious. I prayed to the Lord to help me and teach me how to surrender my situation over to him. The more I prayed for my family to overcome the crack cocaine ordeal, the more my outlook on life in my home became bearable all because I went back to the *Shepherd* and asked for help. Father help me! WOW! These powerful words have made such a significant impact on my life. My wants and needs did not matter to me anymore once I turned them over to the *Shepherd,* I let go and let *God*. It was too much for me to handle the drug situation in my family anymore. *To God be the Glory.*

"He makes me lie down in green pastures: he leadeth me beside the still waters" (Psalm 23:2, KJV)

When I learned how to pray and asked the Lord for help in dealing with a crack addict by turning it over to the *Shepherd,* I began to see brighter days even in the midst of the addiction. Now there was a sense of peace when I was at home with Lucious. I knew the *Shepherd* was working for me and Lucious while we were beginning to lie down in the greener pastures. The arguing stopped, and we looked forward to going to church and fellowshipping with the members. By this time, Lucious noticed the boys and I were attending church during the weekday and on Sundays. As I listened to the sermon as the pastor preached, the words resonate with me as I reflected on what I was going through in my home. The most peaceful times for me were going to church and sitting in the sanctuary alone while everyone else was in their class-rooms. Oh, what peace it brought to my soul!

Months later, while sitting in the sanctuary, the pastor noticed and encouraged me to let go and release my problems. I told him I was tired sitting in the sanctuary brought me the peace I so longed for. All I could think about were the times I had wanted to make Lucious suffer because of the embarrassments he had put us through. But then I remembered how the *Shepherd* had brought me out of harm and danger. Being still at this time was just what I needed. He says, *"Be still and know that I am God. I will be exalted among the nations, I will be exalted in the earth." (Psalm 46:10, NIV)* . Understanding what stillness meant to me was not having control over my trials and tribulations in the first place. I realize I needed to be taken out of this dangerous environment and placed in a calm area to relive the stress I have endured.

I was raised by my grandmother in the Liberty City projects of Miami. She would take me to church over on 18th Avenue. As a child, I watched them worship the Lord at church all day while the kids were sitting in the back of the church asleep or playing with each other. The church sanctuary brought me peace. I remembered when I was with my grandmother when she attended church, and I love her dearly for taking me. Now, I have learned to allow the Lord to lead me, as I began to sit still through the remaining of my ordeal with a crack addict. While taking care of the boys, going to work and church, and no longer arguing with Lucious meant a sense of the peace began to fill my days.

"He restored my soul: he leadeth me in the paths of righteousness for his name's sake" (Psalm 23:3, KJV)

The boys and I finally joined the local neighborhood church after attending there for a year. Lucious joined years later. I began to yearn for the Word for God, because it brought peace into my home. I started attending Bible study and teacher's meetings to learning more about the Word of God as an adult and what it meant to be a Christian. It opened up my eyes to what I was doing wrong in my walk with the *Shepherd*, I had not allowed Him to take care of the boys and me, instead, I was doing things myself. I was lost going through the motion in life, without any directions, just taking one day at a time. I was frustrated with my marriage and trying to get back at Lucious, but getting nowhere. By listening, reading, and studying the Word of God, it all started to become clear. If I would have stayed on course with the *Shepherd* and looked to His commandments, His Word, I would have saved myself years of pain and heartache. My heart and mind had to be restored so I could listen to the *HIS* Word instructing me when to move, when to stop and most of all when to listen to *His* command.

WOW! I missed the mark on what I was supposed to do as a Christian for all those years dealing with a crack addict.

I asked the *Shepherd* to forgive me of my sins knowingly and unknowingly, and guide my walk in a Christian manner. My heart needed to be fixed by *Him* because it was difficult to follow His path and directions, due to the worldly were going on in my family. Trying to handle what the world had to offer caused me to stray away from the very one who created the world -- the *Shepherd*. As a mother raising two boys, my only focus was surviving by any means necessary; I got off on the service road of life but went nowhere.

Service Road of Life

By
Avis Lamb Brown

I got off on the service road of life

Heartaches, pain, suffering, hurt and strife

Heading toward life's uncertainty that it did bring

Trials, tribulations, pain, aches and unimaginable things

How do I handle life without the *Shepherd* to lead and guide me?

Lord, I surrender all and pray to Thee

Cleanse me, guide me, day by day

To fulfill Your will work in every way

My family outlook on life was better once we started focusing on the *Shepherd* and His will. We are all attending church together, and Lucious is a deacon and the youth director.

"Yea, though I walk through the valley of the shadow of death, I will fear no evil: for thou art with me; thy rod and thy staff they comfort me" (Psalm 23:4, KJV).

Reflecting over the years dealing with Lucious crack addiction and walking out of the house when the drug dealer would stop by, I realize I was putting myself in harm's way so many times. When I would follow Lucious outside after the drug dealer blew his car horn I thought my presence would scare them and they would leave. It never happened. After learning about the Word of God and realizing I was in the shadow of death by trying to interfere with the purchase of a drug sale, there was no way I was going to stop their drug transactions. I was fed up with Lucious bringing drug dealers to our home and into the neighborhood. Lucious showed no remorse by doing so.

One evening when Lucious' car broke down, and he needed a tow, he called and asked me to contact the towing service. He gave me the address where his car was located. However, the area where his car had broken down was a well-known area as the most dangerous drug-infested neighborhood in Dallas; there was a strong possibility a towing service would not pick up. After waiting hours for a tow truck to arrive, the driver (a black man) said the reason they took so long was because there were no black drivers available when the call came in, so they waited until one came on duty. I was not thinking about the dangerous areas. I was only trying to help Lucious get his car towed, regardless of what he had done to the boys and me. Was it the right thing to do? I do not know, but I just reacted out of concern, irrespective of what Jr. had to say about me helping Lucious. When Jr. and I arrived where the car was broken down, there was noise and the smell of cigarettes and alcohol. I did not feel threatened in any way; in fact, we were getting to know other parts of Dallas. We just happened to be in one of the most dangerous drug infested areas trying to tow Lucious's car.

This reminded me of one of the dangerous situations when Steven would go with Lucious. He said he was taking Steven to the movies, but ended up at a crack house aka trap house. He took him several times to a crack house when they were supposed to go to the movies and told him to say they went to the movie theater if I asked. Lucious would go inside the crack house to smoke crack and tell Steven to go outside and play in the yard. I thank my *Shepherd* for keeping His arms of protection around Steven and not allowing the desire for someone to do harm or approach him in a dangerous way just to buy crack. Oh, *To God be the Glory*!

Dealing with a crack addict's frame of mind was very unpredictable regardless of their surroundings. How do you analyze or predict the actions of a crack user? I was not a doctor or nurse, just Steven's mother. I was trying to allow Lucious, Steven's father, to spend some time with him, but he only desired to feed his habit. When I stopped following the *Shepherd* and went on my way in this lost world, things and harmful situations came my way. If I had stayed focused on the *Shepherd,* He would have led me and comforted me during this ordeal. I tried to get comfort from my family members out of state, friends, and co-workers, but they just talked about me. I felt I was all alone, for so many years, until I started going to church and asking the *Shepherd* to help me. He was right there along.

Sometimes I felt threatened and in a dangerous situation dealing with a crack addict. Throughout the years while Lucious was on crack, his entire body appearance had changed. He showed senseless and heartless actions toward me, especially when the boys were around. However, the *Shepherd* was with me; His rod and staff comforted me by protecting us and not allowing any physical harm against us. Yes, there was mental abuse, but the *Shepherd* kept me in my right mind as we said terrible things to each other. When I visited the prison near Houston, Texas, the *Shepherd* showed me how I could have ended up in jail if I brought any harm to Lucious. *To God be the Glory*. My bringing harm to Lucious would have caused me to give up my life for prison, and that is never worth the cost of freedom.

I surrender all to the *Shepherd* because *He* knows all and sees all, and He will show you His awesome power in your life regardless of what you are going through. My analogy when the *Shepherd* says, "He is the rod" is when He brings us back to Him at *HIS* given time. When He brings us back to Him, He may not come when you want Him but when you are ready and looking to make a change in your life just call on the *Shephard*. Some make it back to the *Shepherd,* and some do not. Regardless of our setbacks in life, the *Shepherd* is always there waiting for us to ask for help.

"Thou preparest a table before me in the presence of mine enemies: thou anointest my head with oil; my cup runneth over" (Psalm 23:5, KJV).

Once my family and I surrendered all to the *Shepherd* and focused on doing His will, I began to see His work and love in Lucious and our actions toward one other. Who do you consider the enemy when there are drugs involved that have torn your family apart? The *Shepherd* will take care of my enemies before they try to harm me, He will intervene and work things out. As He prepares the table before you sometimes you can see it with the physical eye. However, the table has already been made. We have to trust and believe in God to receive the blessing He has waiting for us. He prepared a table before me during the crack addiction ordeal within my family. I can now see *His* preparations, in the following situations:

- ✓ The Lord kept my family safe while we were in the midst of the storm.
- ✓ Lucious and I never exchanged any harmful or physical contact only words.
- ✓ The Lord was preparing me as the leader of our house to show the boys how to deal with one of life's challenges.
- ✓ The Lord kept us in our right minds regardless of our resentment toward Lucious.
- ✓ The boys and I were still able to enjoy life in the midst of confusion.
- ✓ My family never went without the necessities of life food, shelter, clothing, and transportation.
- ✓ When I had enough of trying to succeed on my own, I prayed to the Lord for help.

From my perspective, *"thou preparest a table before me"* is being seated at a physical table and setting. However, . . . *"in the presence of mine enemies"* illustrates we are going to be seated with many people who will dislike us for various reasons. Remember how Judas betrayed Jesus even though he broke bread with *Him* at the table prepared for the disciples. If Jesus experienced jealousy, envy, and strife during *His* time on earth in human form, so will we. Nevertheless, we must keep our focus on Jesus, and everything will be all right. To God be the Glory!

If the *Shepherd* "anointest my head will with oil, my cup runneth over." The Lord gave me something significant such as knowledge, wisdom, and understanding of His Word as I began to seek His help. The cup runneth over fulfilling needs and wants. The entire time the boys and I were going through trials in our ordeal, we never lacked for anything because the Lord provided. There is nothing capable of holding back what the Lord provides for you. *His* awesome love supersedes our human understanding. The analogy of "my cup runneth over" is that we have experienced in some way a cup running over with something, liquid or solid. So, in essence, He provides ALL we need from a liquid perspective is to drink, take a shower, or wash and water things, from a solid perspective food or any solid item to be used for any solid usage.

"Surely, goodness and mercy shall follow me all the days of my life: and I will dwell in the house of the Lord forever" *(Psalm 23:6, KJV)*.

Two angels are following me all the days of my life: Grace, and Mercy. He gives you Grace and Mercy every day of your life; great is Thou faithfulness. During the time Lucious started committing adultery, it led him to using crack cocaine. The Lord allowed Grace and Mercy to provide for the boys and me without us realizing our blessing. I was caught in the practical action of trying to handle each situation and events Lucious brought my way. I did not concentrate on the Lord until I had enough and when the crack cocaine ordeal was too much for me to handle.

Once I began to pray and turn our problems over to the Lord, I could see and taste the goodness of how He turned a negative experience for many years into a positive one. Lucious and I both continued to live in the same house, and the Lord changed our attitudes toward each other. We can receive the goodness of His works in our lives as He continues to prepare a table for all of us. One day when I exit this earth, I will live in the house of the Lord and dwell in a safer home with Him where there are many mansions. This home will be a place where there is no more suffering in the body and hunger will cease to exist.

While here on earth we have to endure suffering until we dwell with our Lord. Focusing on the Lord will allow us to face the pain a little easier. Once I began and continued to focus on the Lord, during many dark days in my journey while dealing with a drug user. However, the brighter days outweighed the darker days. Earthly issues such as coping with Lucious and his crack addiction, brought pain, embarrassment, and shame. If you stay focused on the Lord, and you can weather the storm's pain. I was not focusing on the Lord until years had passed, and I had faced many obstacles and issues I could not handle. I began to cry out to the Lord, and He heard my cry. *To God be the Glory.*

Chapter Seven

What are your thoughts after reading Chapter Seven?

_____
_____
_____
_____
_____
_____
_____
_____
_____
_____

Have you ever experienced this in your family?

_____
_____
_____
_____
_____
_____
_____
_____
_____
_____

Do you know someone who is going through a similar situation?

_____
_____
_____
_____
_____
_____

What can you do to help or how can you be of support to an abuser?

My thoughts about Chapter Seven - God is showing the family" *Love is patient, love is kind. It does not envy, it does not boast, it is not proud. It does not dishonor others, it is not self-seeking, it is not easily angered, it keeps no record of wrongs. Love does not delight in evil but rejoices with the truth. It always protects, always trusts, always hopes, always perseveres"*
(1 Corinthians 13:4-7, NIV).

Who do we blame, if anyone?

Do you believe in God? Has he brought you out of life situations that you needed to escape? Share your testimony.

_____

_____

_____

_____

_____

_____

_____

_____

_____

_____

"But thanks be to God, which giveth us the victory through our Lord Jesus Christ. Therefore, my beloved brethren, be ye stedfast, unmoveable, always abounding in the work of the Lord, forasmuch as ye know that your labour is not in vain in the Lord" (**1 Corinthians 15:57-58, KJV).**

CHAPTER **8**

A Victorious Act of God
Within Our Family

THE ACT OF God continues to work in and through our family as each of the children began to seek careers in college or the armed forces. Oh, how grateful we are for God's goodness and mercy shown to us dealing with and overcoming a crack addict. Second Corinthians 2:14, (NASB), says *"But thanks be to God, who always leads us in triumph in Christ, and manifest through us the sweet aroma of the knowledge of Him in every place."* The Lord was in every place. We needed Him to carry us through the entire ordeal we thought we could handle. One of my biggest fears was the well-being of my children following the drug addiction experience.

However, God's amazing grace allowed our family to endure and overcome the negativity that drugs can bring to a family. As we prayed and worked together, God gave our family the strength to press on regardless of the situation. When nothing else worked, *His,* love lifted us, and each day delivered a new beginning to work on our careers. Every member of our family decided not to allow the negativity to keep us from thriving as we continued in our careers, we trusted God in our daily walk. *Trust in the Lord with all your heart and lean not to your own understanding: in all your ways submit to him, and he will make your paths straight" (**Proverbs 3:5-6, NIV**).*

Lucious

Lucious and Carrie are still married and living in the same house where all the addiction experiences occurred. Lucious' Christian walk began with his mother praying for God to remove his drug desires. She has always been able to go before God on his behalf when he was unable or unwilling. As she began to feed him with her love, the kind of love that only a mother can give the Holy Spirit began to convict Lucious. The desire immediately left him. She told Lucious "Our God is not slack concerning His promises, just ask, and He will answer." She reminded him to return to a Bible teaching church. God had already placed his wife and kids in such a church. He joined and was mentored by some of the most influential men of God he had ever met. They challenged him to study God's Word through Bible study and goodwill meetings. The brotherhood meetings were the most important and fulfilling times of his Christian journey. As he grew in the knowledge of our Lord and Savior, something began to happen within him.

Lucious had replaced his passion for drugs with the love of God's Word. God's Word became his new addiction. When the Holy Spirit manifested God's Word as Lucious prayed and studied, it became the one thing he had been missing in his life. No longer concealed, but now revealed. It continues to be the standard upon which he tries to live. *"Brethren, I count not myself to have apprehended: but this one thing I do, forgetting those things which are behind, and reaching forth unto those things which are before. If I press toward the mark for the prize of the high calling of God in Christ Jesus"(**Philippians 3:13-14, KJV**).*

"The Lord is my shepherd; I shall not want. He maketh me to lie down in green pastures: he leadeth me beside the still waters. He restoreth my soul: he leadeth me in the paths of righteousness for his

name's sake. Yea, though I walk through the valley of the shadow of death, I will fear no evil: for thou art with me; thy rod and thy staff they comfort me. Thou preparest a table before me in the presence of mine enemies: thou anointest my head with oil; my cup runneth over. Surely goodness and mercy shall follow me all the days of my life: and I will dwell in the house of the Lord forever" **(Psalm 23, KJV).**

Carrie

Years of working in food service as a general manager, Carrie decided to change careers and become a college professor. After pursuing several degrees, Master of Science degrees in Management at Florida Institute of Technology (FIT) and Economics at TAMU-Commerce. Carrie started a teaching career at CTC-Killeen- Gatesville, DCCCD in Dallas, TCCD in Ft. Worth, MCC in Waco and is currently an economics professor at a local college in Waxahachie, Texas. Her career includes teaching college classes at Gatesville prison units, youth village in Dallas, and face-to-face, online and dual credit classes throughout the DFW area. Carrie attributes her knowledge, skills and abilities to accepting Christ at a very young age. Other contributions include her experiences at a historical Black college in Texas, joining Zeta Phi Beta Sorority, and serving in the Army National Guard. Carrie's life desire is to continue to be a servant of God and allow His light to shine in her to see His good works through her and her daily walk. *"Thy word is a lamp unto my feet, and a light unto my path"* **(Psalm 119:105, KJV).**

Jr.

After Jr. graduated from Skyline High School, he attended the University of Tampa in Florida earning a Bachelor of Science degree. He later joined the army and became a captain in logistics. After serving in the military for ten years and experiencing the Iraq war, he decided to end his career as a soldier to pursue teaching college as a finance professor. Jr. went back to college to seek several Master of Science degrees in finance at TAMU-Commerce and Florida Institute of Technology. He earned a Ph.D. in Business Administration and continued his teaching career. He wrote a finance textbook which is now being used in his college finance class. Some of his teaching career began at MCC in Waco, CTC in Killeen- Gatesville prison, MHB in Belton, Texas and currently in ADA, Oklahoma. Jr. attributes his knowledge, skills, and abilities in teaching finance to hard work and dedication to be the best he can be, and in trusting and believing in God to handle any obstacles he may face. He enjoys his family and career. One of his favorite Scriptures is *"What good is it, my brothers and sisters, if someone claims to have faith but has no deeds? Can such faith save them?"* (**James 2:14, NIV**).

Steven

Steven followed in his older brother's footsteps and graduated from Skyline High School in 2001. He was awarded a three-year Army Reserve Officers Training Corps program scholarship to attend the University of Tampa in Florida. He spent the next four years growing personally and professionally while living hundreds of miles away from home. He graduated and was commissioned as a second lieutenant into the Florida Army National Guard in 2005. Steven currently holds the rank of Major as an Operation Training Officer for 1-153 Cavalry Squadron in Panama City, Florida. While deployed to Camp Arifjan, Kuwait in 2010, he pursued a Master of Science degree in General Administration at Central Michigan University. Steven developed some of his leadership skills from the Phi Beta Sigma fraternity. He attributes his knowledge, skills, ability, and successful career to trusting and believing in God. Steven has developed the gift to be an active encourager while leading his soldiers, family, and friends. One of his favorite Scriptures is, *"Work willingly at whatever you do, as though you were working for the Lord rather than for people"* (**Colossians 3:23, NLT**).

Danielle

Danielle was born after Lucious became free from crack cocaine and only remembers her home life, family stories, and reading the first version of my book. However, Danielle admires her family accomplishments and plans to pursue higher education after graduating from Booker T. Washington in Dallas. Her college experience began at Eastfield College in Mesquite with a General Studies Associate's Degree in General Studies, Iowa State in Ames, Iowa and Texas Tech in Lubbock, Texas. She enjoys reading and journaling which led to pursuing a Bachelor of Arts degree in technical writing and English at Texas Tech (Fall 2018). Danielle graduated magna cum laude. She has published her first international article Oryx & Crake Representations with (IJHSSE) as an undergraduate student. Her next educational goal is to obtain a Master of Science in English at TAMU-Commerce, Commerce, Texas. She attributes her knowledge, skills, and abilities to the desire to persevere and overcome any obstacle she faces. Also, Danielle aspires to make an impact on the world around her with one article at a time. *"Train up a child in the way he should go: and when he is old, he will not depart from it"* **(Proverbs 22:6, KJV).**

Chapter Eight

What are your thoughts after reading Chapter Eight?

_____

_____

_____

_____

_____

_____

_____

_____

_____

_____

Have you ever experienced this in your family?

_____

_____

_____

_____

_____

_____

_____

_____

_____

_____

Do you know someone who has overcame a drug abuser?

_____

_____

_____

_____

_____

_____

_____
_____
_____

What can you do to help or how can you be of support to an abuser?
_____
_____
_____
_____
_____
_____
_____
_____
_____
_____

My thoughts about Chapter Eight - God is showing the family, *"For the Lord your God is the one who goes with you to fight for you against your enemies to give you victory"* (**Deuteronomy 20: 4, NIV**).

What was the outcome of an abuser in your family?
_____
_____
_____
_____
_____
_____
_____
_____
_____
_____

Do you believe in God and has He brought you out of life situations you needed to escape? Share your testimony.

_____

_____

_____

_____

_____

_____

_____

_____

_____

_____

_____

"For everyone born of God overcomes the world. This is the victory that has overcome the world, even our faith" **(1 John 5:4, NIV).**

All You Need Is Faith

By
Avis Lamb Brown

When a life uncertainty attempts to break me down

Can you help me, somebody, anybody, no one seems to be around?

How can I focus on the Word that God left for me to read?

The drugs make me feel so good that I allow it to take the lead

I have turned my back on God for so long

Every turn I try to make it right, it seems that it goes wrong

Momma says to pray each and every day

The world's temptations are real, so hard to deal with in every way

Lord, I surrender all to You

This sinful life alone is too hard to deal;
Lord I need You to bring me through

Lord, I surrender all to You, only you, please make a way

My child, my child all you need is Faith

"Now, faith, is the substance of things hoped for, the evidence of things not seen" **(Hebrews 11:1, KJV).**

The Lord is Our Shepherd

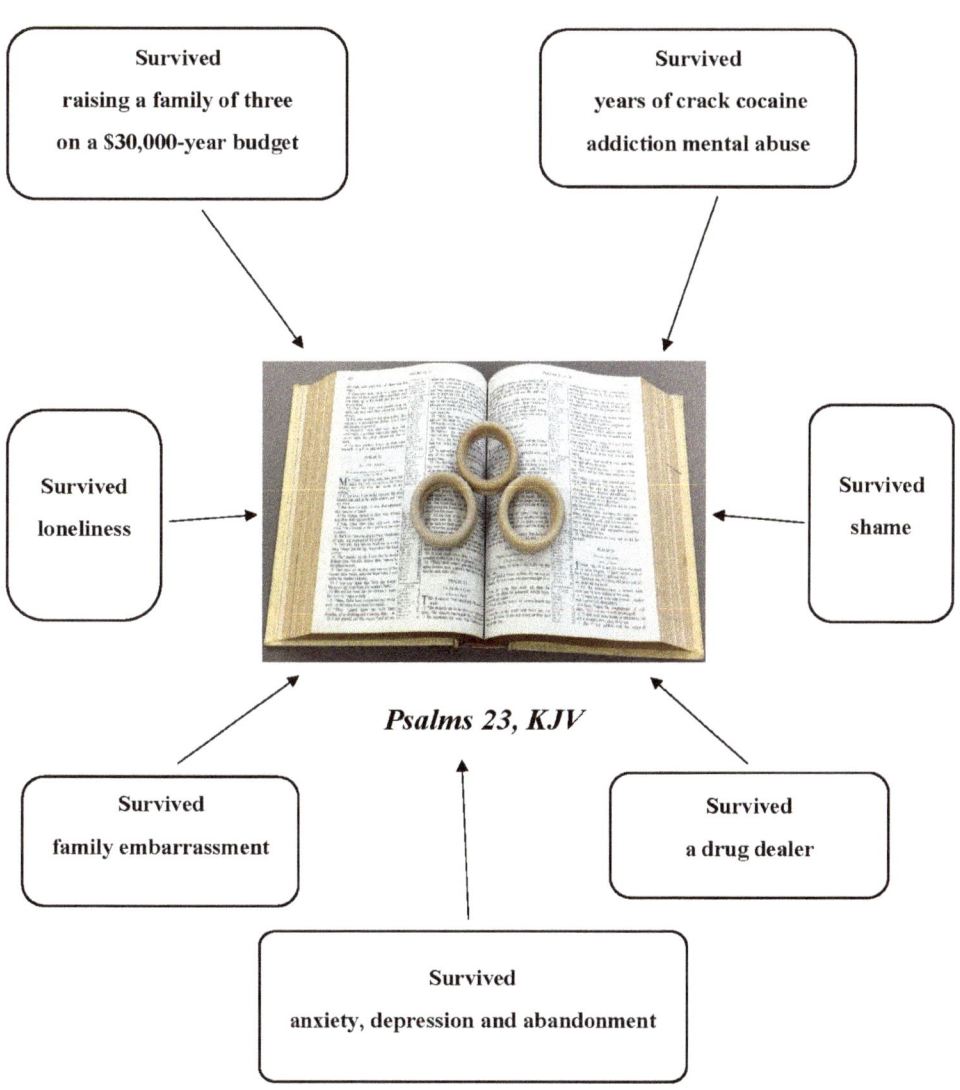

Survived raising a family of three on a $30,000-year budget

Survived years of crack cocaine addiction mental abuse

Survived loneliness

Survived shame

Survived family embarrassment

Survived a drug dealer

Survived anxiety, depression and abandonment

Psalms 23, KJV

My Friend, My Lover, My Husband Triumphant Reflection

My Friend

My friend became my heavenly Father who heard all of my worries, complaints, and cries. I believed it was my mother, but she could only listen to me when we talked on the telephone. I considered my co-workers and neighbors as my friends, but they honestly did not understand what I was going through in my heart and mind unless I shared my feelings with them. This crack cocaine ordeal lasted for years. Every time I would try to reach out to someone, their body language resisted hearing more of the Lucious stories. Sometimes I would talk to myself into continuing to put up with his illness.

When I turned to the Lord, I began to understand and see who my friend was all those years. However, I never talked to Him or reached out to Him like I did my mother, neighbor or co-workers. I was running in circles trying to put out fires or hide shameful acts Lucious did day and night. Lucious, I even thought Lucious was my friend during the years we were making plans for our future together, turns out I was wrong. The Lord kept us together in the same house throughout the drug addiction. We began to understand what a true friend is all about from a biblical perspective. *"Do not forsake your friend or a friend of your family, and do not go to your relative's house when disaster strikes you better a neighbor nearby than a relative far away"* (**Proverbs 27:10, NIV**).

My Lover

After years of being together, Lucious and I developed a love relationship for one another that grew from a friendship. We tried to make it work based on the family values which were instilled in us. There were times when we would visit each other at the family homes. You were not allowed to share a bed together if you were not husband and wife. Prior to our visits, we had to go through the parents for permission, and they had to give their blessing on the sleeping arrangement. The conversations we shared with each other about unique things were kept between us. Also, holding hands was not permitted around the families.

You can say we were lovers behind closed doors because of the do's and don'ts that were not allowed in public and outside of the immediate family. Our family values taught us how to respect each other as a person, not exposing ourselves in a manner that would embarrass the family name. My mother did not share the specific conversation about being in a relationship or lovers; my father was deceased when I became an adult. Therefore, how to love each other in a relationship, in most cases, was left up to us to follow our feelings.

The Bible teaches us how to love because God loved us first by sending His only Son to save us from the consequences of sin. There is no greater love. Christ left the Bible as our instruction book to read and follow as a single or married person. Love is an action word, and Lucious and I fell short of that action when we were going through the drug ordeal. Once we cried for Christ's help, He took time to teach both of us every day about love. Inviting the Lord into our marriage again was the very best move we would ever make in our relationship and life. We weathered the storm, we endured the hardships, and we saw the light at the end of the tunnel. *"For God so loved the world, that he gave his only begotten Son,* *that whosoever believeth in him should not perish, but have ever-lasting life" **(John 3:16, KJV).***

My Husband

When Lucious and I decided to get married, we were a couple at the Christian college in Texas. Getting married was a norm back in the day. If you were dating for several years; marriage was expected, and relationships were taken seriously. The asking of the hand in marriage was part of the man's responsibility if he wanted to marry his girlfriend. Family values were upheld, and we were taught how to respect one another in a relationship.

I often thought a man's role was significant in the family. He provided for the entire family and was upon as the leader. When we married and started a family, I do not recall referring to the Bible for instruction. Instead, Lucious looked up to his father for guidance and words of wisdom. God is holding the man accountable for leading and raising the family, and if he falls short of that, the family fails as well. When Lucious turned his back on the boys and me for many years, I wondered if he was ready for the task of being the head of the family as ordained by God.

Once Lucious started going to church and attending Bible study with some of the older deacons, there was a change in his walk and talk toward the family. He started to look in the Word of God for guidance on how to become a father and husband to us. Even though his birth father was still alive, he had forgotten about his heavenly Father, our Lord and Savior for guidance. We both endured difficulties in our marriage without consulting the Lord. When Lucious took his position as husband, God restored our marriage.

"Marriage should be honored by all, and the marriage bed kept pure, for God will judge the adulterer and all the sexually immoral. Keep your lives free from the love of money and be content with what you have, because God has said,

'Never will I leave you;
Never will I forsake you.'
So we say with confidence,
'The Lord is my helper; I will not be afraid' **(Hebrews 13:4-6, NIV).**

List of Divine Scriptures Throughout the Story

THE WORD OF God is a divine message to use in our everyday life. All the Scriptures used in this story are to remind us that if we stay connected to the Word of God during our trials, and tribulations of life, He will bring us through just as He did with our family. So often we try to fix our problems and end up causing more harm to our entire family unit. When we have done all we can do, then we want to turn it over to God.

- 2 Corinthians 5:7, (NKJV)
- Hebrews 11:1, (KJV)
- Exodus 34:4, (KJV)
- Exodus 20:3, (NKJV)
- Genesis 1:11, (KJV)
- Mark 8:36, (KJV)
- Ephesians 5:6-18, (ESV)
- 1 Peter 5:8, (KJV)
- Proverbs 25:28, (NIV)
- Philippians 3:19, (ESV)
- Philippians 4:7, (ESV)

In the beginning was the Word, and the Word was with God, and the Word was God (**John 1:1, KJV**).

- John 20:21-22, (ESV)
- Matthew 6:33, (KJV)
- Matthew 26:11, (NLT)
- Romans 8:28, (NIV)
- Colossians 3:19, (KJV)
- 1 Timothy 5:8, (KJV)
- 1 Timothy 6:10, (KJV)
- Deuteronomy 32:35, (NASB)
- 1 John 2:15, (KJV)
- Hebrews 13:4, (ESV)
- Ephesians 5:23-25, (KJV)
- Romans 12:19, (NASB)
- Job 7:11, (KJV)
- John 16:33, (NKJV)

"Trust in the Lord with all your heart and lean not on your own under-standing; in all your ways submit to him, and he will make your path straight" (**Proverbs 3:5-6, NIV**).

- Galatians 5:19-21, (NIV)
- Isaiah 42:19-21, (NIV)
- Romans 10:1, (KJV)
- Matthew 5:38-39, (KJV)
- Romans 12:21, (KJV)
- Ephesians 6:12, (ESV)
- Matthew 11:28-30, (NIV)
- Psalm 55:22, (KJV)
- Proverbs 3:5-6, (NASB)
- 1 Corinthians 13:7, (KJV)
- Colossians 3:21, (KJV)
- Matthew 5:44, (KJV)
- Galatians 5:19, (KJV)
- Ephesians 6:11-12, (KJV)

The Word serves as God's spokesman. Jesus said that HE performed this role: *"For I did not speak on my own, but the Father who sent me commanded me to say all that I have spoken. So, whatever I say is just what the Father has told me to say"* (***John 12:49-50, NIV).***

- Psalm 30:5, (KJV)
- 1 Timothy 6:10, (KJV)
- 1 Corinthians 6:19-20, (KJV)

- 2 Timothy 1:7, (KJV)
- James 4:7, (KJV)
- 2 Timothy 2:25-26, (NLT)
- John 14:27, (KJV)
- Psalm 23:4, (ESV)
- Psalm 27:1, (ESV)
- Psalm 55:22, (KJV)
- Philippians 4:6, (NASB)
- Romans 8:28, (NKJV)
- Deuteronomy 31:6, (KJV)

The Word came to earth as a human. The Word is God's Son, Jesus Christ. We had a view of HIS glory. *"And the Word was made flesh, and dwelt among us, (and we beheld his glory, the glory as of the only begotten of the Father,) full of grace and truth"* (**John 1:14, KJV).**

- Matthew 6:33, (KJV)
- Psalm 34:6, (ESV)
- Matthew 25:37, (KJV)
- 1 Corinthians 10:13, (KJV)
- Hebrews 13:4, (ISV)
- Psalm 126:5, (KJV)
- Romans 8:35–36, (NIV)
- Matthew 6:31-34, (NKJV)
- 1 Peter 5:6-10, (ESV)
- Psalm 52:2, (ESV)
- John 16:33, (NIV)

- Isaiah 54:17, (KJV)
- Proverbs, 6:16-19, (ESV)
- Psalm 46:1, (ESV)

"But as many as received Him, to them He gave the right to become children of God, to those who believe in His name" ***(1 John 1:11-12, NKJV).***

- 2 Thessalonians 3:3, (ESV)
- 1 Corinthians 3:17, (ESV)
- Psalm 147:3, (NKJV)
- Psalm 5:11, (NLT)
- Proverbs 3:5-6, (KJV)
- Psalm 23:1, (KJV)
- Isaiah 40:31, (KJV)
- Psalm 27:1, (KJV)
- Deuteronomy 31:6, (ESV)
- Proverbs 3:5, (ESV)
- Proverbs 16:24, (KJV)
- Ecclesiastes 3:4-8, (KJV)
- Romans 12:19, (KJV)
- Galatians 6:3-4, (KJV)

"All things were made by him; and without him was not any thing made that was made"
(John 1:3, (KJV).

- Psalm 147:3, (KJV)
- 1 Peter 5:7-11, (NASB)
- Isaiah 54:17, (KJV)
- Matthew 16:26, (NIV)
- 1 Corinthians 6:19, (NIV)
- Psalm 102:1, (NKJV)
- 1 Timothy 5:8, (NIV)
- Romans 7:21, (KJV)
- Matthew 7:15, (KJV)
- Lamentations 3:22-23, (KJV)
- Proverbs 22:6, (KJV)
- Matthew 15:19, (ISV)
- Romans 12:2, (KJV)
- Philippians 4:19, (KJV)

"I write these things to you who believe in the name of the Son of God so that you may know that you have eternal life" **(1 John 5:13, NLV).**

- 2 Corinthians 6:4-5, (NLT)
- Matthew 16:18, (KJV)
- Proverbs 3:5-6, (ESV)
- Matthew 18:21-22, (NIV)
- Matthew 10:19, (KJV)

- Isaiah 41:10, (KJV)
- Psalm 121:7-8, (ESV)
- Matthew 5:38-40, (NASB)
- 1 John 4:8-9, (KJV)
- Hebrews 4:12, (NIV)
- 1 John 4:7-21, (NIV)
- 2 Corinthians 12:9, (NIV)
- 2 Samuel 16:12, (NIV)
- Philippians 4:13, (ESV)

"For God so loved the world that h gave his one and only Son, that whoever believes in him shall not perish but have eternal life" **(John 3:16, ESV).**

- Psalm 18:2, (NASB)
- Romans 12:2, (NIV)
- John 16:33, (NIV)
- Hebrews 4:16, (NIV)
- Lamentations 3:22-24, (NIV)
- Psalm 51:1, (NIV)
- Romans 12:2, (NIV)
- Psalm 23:1, (KJV)
- Psalm 23:2, (KJV)
- Psalm 23:3, (KJV)
- Psalm 23:4, (KJV)
- Psalm 23:5, (KJV)

- Psalm 23:6, (KJV)
- 1 Corinthians 13:4-7, (KJV)

"Who is it that overcomes the world? Only the one who believes that Jesus is the Son of God" **(1 John 5:5, NIV).**

- 1 Corinthians 15:57-58, (KJV)
- John 15:11, (KJV)
- Proverbs 3:5-6, (NIV)
- Psalm 23, (KJV)
- Psalm 119:105, (KJV)
- Colossians 3:23, (NLT)
- Proverbs 22:6, (KJV)
- Deuteronomy 20:4, (NIV)
- 1 John 5:4, (KJV)
- Hebrews 11:1, (KJV)
- Proverbs 27:10, (NIV)
- John 3:16, (KJV)
- Hebrews 13:4-6, (NIV)
- Psalm 46:10, (NIV)

Joy and Pain of the Heart

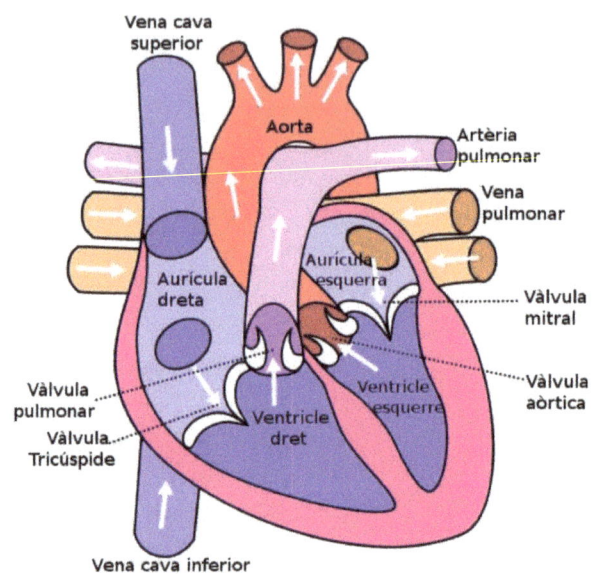

JOY AND PAIN are a part of life that a person must experience; no one will escape the pleasures and pains life experiences will bring. Just as blood flows in and out through the human heart, so does the happiness of joy and the heartaches of sorrow. The human heart continues to pump as it was designed to do, regardless of the emotions of a person. But how much can a person endure of life's pain and suffering, then switch to enjoying the happy times it also brings? Some people give up and allow the pain to dictate their lives. Some let go and let God. *"But the fruit of the Spirit is love, joy, peace, longsuffering, gentleness, goodness, faith, Meekness, temperance: against such there is no law"* (Galatians 5:22-23, KJV). Divine Scriptures used throughout the book brought comfort and understanding to Carrie. She began to realize her limitations regarding the family's joy and pain within the household. She questioned numerous times how a family could handle the emotional stress inflicted by crack cocaine. Carrie turned it over to God and began to see His peace flourish among the family. *"These things have I spoken unto you, that my joy might remain in you, and that your joy might be full"* (**John 15:11, KJV**).

Acknowledgements

THE REWRITE OF *My Friend, My Lover, My Husband*, was inspired by listening to the gospel of Proverbs preached by Pastor Turner. In the first book, I shared a story about my family overcoming life with a drug addict. I failed to mention it was God's amazing grace and mercy that carried us and walked with each of my family members daily during the addiction journey. I am grateful for having the will not to allow the crack addiction to take control of my household. Growing up in a Christian home reminded me to pray and believe God would protect my house from the drug addict. I want to thank Pastor Terry M. Turner and his wife, Dr. Nancy Turner, for their spiritual leadership and guidance.

Special thanks to Lenora Summerall Lamb, my mother, for keeping my focus on prayer because the addiction experience was too big for me to handle. I thank God for Pop and Granny's spiritual strength through prayer and support wherever it was needed in our family. To James Franklin, my husband, I thank God as He kept you in his loving arms during your addiction and brought you out of your dependence on a white powdered substance to depending on Him. My oldest son, James Jr., for supporting and helping me in whatever was needed, especially caring for his bother Daniel Steven. To my baby boy, Daniel Steven, God placed you in the lives of Jr. and me to detract us during the addiction experience, I am grateful for both of you as we enjoyed each other's company in the midst of a storm. To my baby girl, Jamesa Danielle, your presence brought new joy to all of our lives as we started the healing process of overcoming athe drug addiction ordeal. Also, to my MFBC sisters in Christ proofreaders Debra Burton, Valerie Gordon, and Yolanda Shade. Lastly, to my family and friends for offering support in kind words and prayer. *To God be the Glory!*

Order Form

Please send me _____ copies of

My Friend, My Lover, My Husband, A Triumphant Experience Dealing with Crack Cocaine

Price (per book):   **$15.99**
Tax per Book: **$1.32**
Shipping & Handling per Book: **$3.00**
Total: **$20.31**

Send Check or Money Order to:
Avis Lamb Brown
P.O. Box 271051
Dallas, Texas 75227

Shipping Information:

Name	
Address	
City	State	Zip
Telephone	

Please make check or money order payable to: **Avis Lamb Brown**

About the Author

AVIS LAMB BROWN wrote and self-published her first book titled, *My Friend, My Lover, My Husband* in 1997. After years of experiencing the Lord's blessing through her faith and family, she decided to rewrite her first book from a triumphant experience dealing with crack cocaine. The rewrite was placed on her heart when she came to realize she had a deeper story to tell. While attending Mesquite Friendship Baptist Church (MFBC), Mesquite, Texas, under the leadership of Pastor Terry Turner, his spiritual and biblical teaching encouraged her to write the new book. Years of witnessing the goodness of God's new Grace and Mercy she wanted to tell *THE* story of how the Lord was always in the midst of her experiences. *To God be the Glory*. Even though her family was dealing with a crack addict for some years, they lost focus on who was in control God. Avis had to put on her seatbelt and allow God to work everything out from the first day until the time James left the drug recovery center after receiving help.

A crack cocaine life had their family in such a turmoil. But when she decided she had enough is when she turned her situation over to God. Once Avis received the Word of God in her heart, HE showed her His love when He gave us His only begotten *SON* so we can live. She questioned herself numerous times and wondered how she would handle the brokenness in her life by turning it over to God. The brokenness between the family members that was created by the drug user took away joy, happiness, security, and love. Having a godly love in her heart and life equipped her to handle the worldly trials and tribulations the family endured throughout the crack addiction experience. *To God be the Glory.*

After months of listening to Pastor Turner's sermons, Avis would tell him afterwards she felt he was talking directly to her. Hearing the Word of God sermons for several months, she felt as if Pastor Turner knew what her family was going through and was assuring her of God's blessing over her household regardless of what happened inside. He would smile and say to her *"To God be the Glory."* Simply put, this went on for about six months during his series in the book of Proverbs. At that time, it was placed on Avis' heart to ask the Pastor to help her rewrite *My Friend, My Lover, My Husband* from a triumphant experience. This Scripture came to mind, *"Be still, and know that I am God; I will be exalted among the nations, I will be exalted in the earth" (***Psalm 46:10, NIV)**

Lightning Source UK Ltd.
Milton Keynes UK
UKHW020910281119
354389UK00006B/154/P